A Companion Anthology to *Literature for Teaching*

Solo Vocal Repertoire for Singers and Teachers of Singers

Bass Edition

by
Christopher Arneson and Lauren Athey-Janka

Inside View Press

Solo Vocal Repertoire for Singers and Teachers of Singers
Bass Edition

by

Christopher Arneson
&
Lauren Athey-Janka

ISBN: 978-0-9910876-7-9

Printed in the United States of America

Inside View Press
Gahanna, Ohio
www.VoxPed.com

Introduction

The intent of this book is to provide tools that will help students and teachers achieve their pedagogic goals. The repertoire we have chosen, along with the technical instructions provided in this book, will guide the teaching of breathing and breath support, phonation, registration, resonance, and articulation. Translations and phonetic transcriptions are provided for each selection to help students explore musical and emotional expression.

For a better understanding of the technical concepts employed in the selection and preparation of the repertoire that is included in this volume, please refer to:

Literature for Teaching: A Guide for Teaching Solo Vocal Repertoire from a Developmental Perspective by Christopher Arneson with Lauren Athey-Janka, Inside View Press, 2014

Acknowledgements

The authors extend their sincerest thanks to the following people:

Nicolette Biddle
Josh Bodanza
Alexander Brousseau
Andrew Gavin
Lauren Gilmore
Vicky Nooe
Mike Parisi
Kathryn Pepe
Elisabeth Pirolli
Robert Sickles
Dan Sullivan

Solo Vocal Repertoire for Singers and Teachers of Singers
Bass Edition

Table of Contents

I.P.A. GUIDE: VOWELS

Forward vowels:	[i]	cheese	***Back vowels:***	[u]	rude
	[I]	hip		[ʊ]	hook
	[e]	hey		[o]	rope
	[ɛ]	wed		[ɔ]	raw
	[æ]	bad		[ɑ]	father
	[a]	mama			

Central vowels:	[ʌ]	up	***Diphthongs:***	[eɪ]	wait
	[ə]	about		[oʊ]	vote
	[ɝ]	heard, American r		[aɪ]	wine
	[ɒ]	dare, British vocalic r		[aʊ]	couch
	[ɚ]	never, American r		[ɔɪ]	joy
				[ju]	huge

Mixed vowels:	[y]	German: *für*	French: lune
	[Y]	German: *Glück*	
	[ø]	German: *schön*	French: deux
	[œ]	German: *könnte*	French: coeur

French Nasals:	[ɛ̃]	[ɛ] plus nasality	French: *bien* [bjɛ̃]
			English: fount**ain**
	[ɑ̃]	[ɑ] plus nasality	French: *dans* [dɑ̃]
			English: ho**n**k
	[õ]	[o] plus nasality	French: *bon* [bõ]
			English: **on**ly
	[œ̃]	[œ] plus nasality	French: *humble* [œ̃blə]
			English: **un**cle

German Diphthongs:	[aɪ]	German: *meine*	English: mine
	[ao]	German: *Augen*	English: couch
	[ɔø]	German: *Freude*	English: joy

Glottal Stop:	[ʔ]	closure of glottis, as in the expression "uh-oh"

I.P.A. GUIDE: CONSONANTS

Stop plosives:			*Nasals:*		[m]	mind
	[p]	pal			[n]	narrow
	[b]	back			[ŋ]	sing
	[t]	teach				
	[d]	down				
	[k]	kangaroo				
	[g]	get				

Fricatives:			*Lateral:*		[l]	laugh
	[f]	finger				
	[v]	victory				
	[θ]	thin				
	[ð]	that				
	[s]	self				
	[z]	zebra				
	[ʃ]	ship				
	[ʒ]	azure				
	[h]	him				

Glides:			*Combined:*		[tʃ]	chip
	[r]	rose (American English)			[dʒ]	jump
	[j]	yellow				
	[ʍ]	what, unvoiced				
	[w]	way, voiced				

Trill, Tap, or flip:		
	[ɾ]	Italian: *moro* (single flip R)
	[r]	Italian: *ride* (trilled R)
	[r. r]	Italian: *terra* (prolonged trilled R)

Enya: [ɲ]   English: onion   Italian: *regno* [reɲɔ]   French: *vignes* [viɲə]

Elya: [ʎ]   English: million   Italian: *figlio* [fiʎɔ]

French Glide: [ɥ]   French: lui [lɥi] (pronounce [y] then quickly move to [i])

German ichlaut: [ç]   English: hue   German: *dich* [diç]

German achlaut: [χ]   German: *nacht* [naχt]

A Basic Guide to Vocal Exercises for Beginning Singing Teachers

The questions we are asked most frequently concern the use and function of vocal exercises, or *vocalises*. These inquiries often come from young, aspiring voice teachers and singers, so it seems appropriate to discuss their application.

One of the main reasons for using vocal exercises is to establish good singing technique. But while singing teachers likely agree that voice training must address issues of posture and alignment, respiration, phonation, registration, resonation, and articulation, there is little consensus about the specific types of exercises that should be used. Vocal exercises themselves have no intrinsic value; their effectiveness is measured by how they are applied and under what conditions they are used. Vocal exercises can be designed to help singers achieve optimal onset (initiation of the tone), placement, resonance, breath support, phrasing, legato, staccato, agility, range, vowel clarity, consonants, intonation, and coordination of registers (consecutive pitches with similar timbre that are produced with the same vocal mechanism).

Pre-phonatory exercises involving relaxation, posture, and alignment are essential. Working with students to free specific areas of tension, including muscles of the jaw, tongue, and neck, and helping them to understand the importance of a well-aligned body is the first order of business (e.g. spine elongated, neck back, sternum out, pelvis tucked under, knees unlocked).

The goal of a balanced **ONSET**, or the easy, clean initiation of tone, is usually achieved with simple exercises that feature repeated notes with a breath in between each repetition. Voiced consonants facilitate resonance, tonal efficiency, and clean, clear onsets. An audible, aspirate [h] often is used in staccato or panting exercise, quickly moving on to an inaudible, or imaginary [h].

PLACEMENT refers to the physical sensations experienced while singing. Exercises involving nasal consonants, the vowels [e] and [i], and staccato exercises using voiced consonants, often are used to increase the awareness of resonance sensations in the mask (the general area of the cheekbones).

Maximizing **RESONANCE** is one of the chief goals of classical singing; humming often is used as exercise for this purpose. The colloquial, affirmative "mm-hmm" and the nasal consonant [ng], often also are used to increase sensations of resonance, along with the sibilants [s] and [z] followed by vowels.

The coordination of expiration and phonation, called **BREATH SUPPORT** (breath management), can be developed through the use of pulsation exercises on repeated notes (e.g. [a, a, a, a]), staccato, and the *messa di voce* (crescendo-decrescendo). Lip trills also help to develop breath management skills, as do voiced sibilant and fricative consonants [z] and [v].

LEGATO is consistent phonation, uninterrupted by changing pitches or words, and is one of the most desirable aspects of beautiful singing. Glissandos (slides) can be helpful in introducing the idea of legato, followed by intervallic skip, slurring between each skip. Changing vowels on a slow scale or repeated tones with a single vowel also are useful exercises.

STACCATO is produced much in the same way as legato but without sustaining the sound between each note. Simple scales and repeated notes with a vowel preceded by [h] or [b] and simple arpeggiated chords using "hip" and "yuh" teach staccato effectively. Staccato exercises also help to develop onset and breath coordination.

PHRASING is the grouping of notes into specific units for an artistic or technical purposes. Exercises that develop legato and breath management can help to teach phrasing. Sustained scales, arpeggios and exercises with strategically placed breaths also develop the breath control skills necessary for long phrases.

AGILITY, the execution of fast moving passages with clear articulation, accuracy, and freedom, promotes flexibility and coordination and is of primary importance in good singing. Fast arpeggios and ascending/descending scales using the vowels [u] and [a] (or alternating vowels) help to develop agility.

RANGE extension is accomplished by singing ascending and descending scales and arpeggios, using five, eight, nine, eleven, and sixteen tones. A variety of vowels can be used alone and in combination.

VOWEL clarity, unification, equalization, differentiation, and evenness also must be taught. The production of a free, consistent scale throughout the vocal range with distinct, clear vowels on every pitch is paramount to good singing (voice acoustics makes this nearly impossible for women singing their highest pitches). A neutral tongue position from which all other vowels can be produced will help to develop vowel clarity. Simple arpeggios that alternate front and back vowels such as [a-o-i-o], also are useful.

CONSONANTS, especially voiced consonants, frequently are used in vocal exercises to develop coordinated onset and resonance. Scale patterns, repeated notes, arpeggios, and thirds are useful, with consonants articulated on every note. Initial, medial, and final consonants should be included, and paired unvoiced and voiced consonants are beneficial. Exercises using consonants help to create freedom and flexibility in the articulators (jaw, tongue, and lips).

Exercises for the **COORDINATION of REGISTERS** to promote a seamless, consistent vocal scale usually begin in the area just above or below the register break or *passaggio*. A vocalise consisting of two pitches moving slowly from one to the next and modulating up and down through the *passaggio* is helpful. A variety of vowels may be used on short scales, followed by short arpeggios and interval skips. Closed vowels often are used for men in the upper *passaggio* (above Middle-C, also known as C^4) and for women in the lower *passaggio* (also above Middle-C). Alternating between the vowels [u] and [a] can help singers coordinate the registers.

Descending arpeggios from the head voice in women and falsetto in men, and the use of sirens (vocal slides) also are beneficial.

Ingo Titze, one of our foremost voice scientists, lists "The Five Best Vocal Warmup Exercises" in Volume 57, No.3, 2001 of the *Journal of Singing*:

- Lip trill and tongue trill
- Two octave pitch glides
- Forward tongue roll and extension
- *Messa di voce* (crescendo-decrescendo)
- Staccato on arpeggios

By taking into account the criteria we use to judge whether a tone is functional and/or beautiful—easy onset, legato, clear diction, bright/dark tone quality, excellent breath management skills—we can make decisions as to which exercises might help students best achieve these goals. Keeping a record of what we see and hear in our initial consultation with a singer can serve as a basis for the vocalises that subsequently are developed and utilized.

Students must understand that a secure singing technique can be achieved through regular use of vocal exercises, which should be described in a simple and objective manner. All exercises should be tailored to serve the needs of individual students; few really are needed, provided every aspect of technique is addressed. Many teachers believe that it is essential to assign a specific sequence of vocal exercises, which often follow the major areas of vocal technique, including posture, respiration, phonation, resonance, support, registration, articulation. While this strategy might prove helpful, it is not required.

There are numerous books of vocalises still in print by the 19th century singing masters, including Sieber, Vaccai, Concone and Marchesi. All were well-known teachers and their exercises, along with those of contemporary authors such as William Vennard, Richard Miller, Oren Brown and James McKinney, can help young teachers get started.

A Vocal Exercise Bibliography

Brown, Oren L. (1996). *Discover Your Voice*. San Diego, CA: Singular Publishing Group, Inc.

Coffin, B. (1980). *Overtones of Bel Canto*. Metuchen, NJ: The Scarecrow Press, Inc.

Concone, J. (1898). *Thirty Daily Exercises for the Voice*. New York: G. Schirmer, Inc.

Garcia, M., II. (1975) *A Complete Treatise on the Art of Singing: Part Two* (D. V. Paschke, Ed. and Trans.). New York: Da Capo Press.

Lamperti, G. B. (1905). *The Techniques of Bel Canto* (M. Heidrich. Ed., T. Baker, Trans.). New York: G. Schirmer.

Marchesi, S. (1970) *Bel Canto: A Theoretical and Practical Vocal Method*. London: Enoch and Sons, Ltd., n.d.; reprint, New York: Dover Publications.

McKinney, J. C. (1982) *The Diagnosis and Correction of Vocal Faults*. Nashville, TN: Broadman Press.

Miller, R. (1986). *The Structure of Singing*. New York: Schirmer Books.

Reid, C. L. (1965). *The Free voice: A Guide to Natural Singing*. New York: Coleman-Ross Company, Inc.

Sieber, Ferdinand (1899). *Thirty-Six Eight-Measure Vocalises for Soprano*: op. 92: Volume 111 of Schirmer's library of music classics.

Sieber, Ferdinand (1899). *Thirty-Six Eight-Measure Vocalises for Mezzo-Soprano*: op. 93: Volume 112 of Schirmer's library of music classics.

Sieber, Ferdinand (1899). *Thirty-Six Eight-Measure Vocalises for Alto*: op. 94: Volume 113 of Schirmer's library of music classics.

Sieber, Ferdinand (1899). *Thirty-Six Eight-Measure Vocalises for Tenor*: op. 95: Volume 114 of Schirmer's library of music classics.

Sieber, Ferdinand (1899). *Thirty-Six Eight-Measure Vocalises for Baritone*: op. 96: Volume 115 of Schirmer's library of music classics.

Sieber, Ferdinand (1899). *Thirty-Six Eight-Measure Vocalises for Bass*: op. 97: Volume 116 of Schirmer's library of music classics.

Vennard, W. (1967). *Singing: The Mechanism and the Technic* (rev. ed.). Boston: Carl Fischer, Inc.

Christopher Arneson & Lauren Athey-Janka

Il Zeffiro

Italian
Vincenzo Bellini

Respiration and Support

Practice ascending leaps on lip trills, starting in the middle voice and working up to the highest pitch in the song. Next, use [v] in the same exercise. Lip trills encourage movement of air and [v] creates balanced air pressure.

Lip Trill

[vvv]

Resonance

To obtain excellent resonance and a stable and flexible laryngeal position, sing the melody of this piece from vowel-to-vowel while maintaining the sensation a yawn.

[ɛ   i   ɛ   e   a   i   ɔ   o   aːi   a]

[ɛ   o a   e   a   ɛ   o   e   e   e   i   iːo   e]

[ɔ   o   i   i̯o   a   o   i   io   ɛ - -]

Phonation

The bass voice tends to be less flexible than other voice types. The modest ornamentation and wide intervallic leaps found in this piece can help to achieve flexibility. Intone the text on a comfortable middle pitch, elongating the vowels and voiced consonants to obtain a smooth transition from syllable to syllable.

I.P.A.

[vvvvɛɛɛnnnn.tiiii.ˈt͡ʃɛɛɛɛllll]

[mmmmiiii:oooo teeee.zzzzɔɔɔɔ:.ɾoooo]

[faaaa.ˈvvvvɛɛɛɛlll.lll.aaaaʎ.ʎiiii]

Registration

Descending triplets will prepare the student for the flexibility required in this piece. Begin with this descending triplet pattern, and then transition to the musical examples that appear below.

Diction/Articulation

This text requires almost no downward movement of the jaw. Place a finger on the chin and let the tongue do the work while slowly speaking the text.

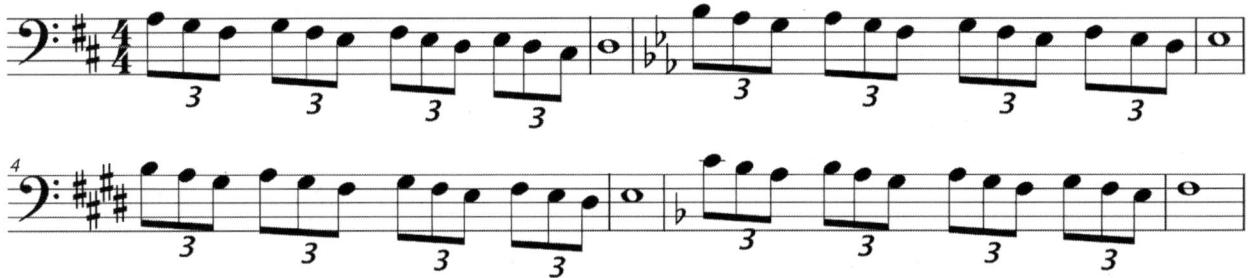

Next, apply the flexibility found in the vocal exercises to these measures of the song.

bat - ten - do a me ___ d'ap - - pres - - - - - - so

Phonetic Transcription and Translation of the Text

Venticel,   che   l'ali   d'oro
[vɛn.ti.ˈt͡ʃɛl   ke   laː.li   ˈdɔː.ɾo]
Little breeze, whose wings of gold

Vai   battendo   a   me   d'appresso,
[vaːi   bat.ˈtɛn.do   a   me   da.ˈprɛs.so]
are beating near to me,

Se   vedesti   il   mia   tesora,
[se   ve.ˈde.‿stil   ˈmiːa   te.ˈzɔː.ɾa]
if you can see the one I treasure,

Dimmi,   o   caro,   dimmi   ov'è.
[ˈdim.mi   o   ˈkaː.ɾo   ˈdim.mi   o.ˈvɛ]
tell me, oh dearest, tell me where he is.

Ah!   se   il   loco ov'ei   soggiorna
[a   se   il   ˈlɔː.‿kov.ˈeːi   sod.ˈd͡ʒor.na]
Ah! if to the place where he dwells

Penetrar   non   m'è concesso,
[pe.ne.ˈtraːr   non   mɛ   kon.ˈt͡ʃɛs.so]
I am not permitted to enter,

Zeffiretto,   a   lui   ritorna
[dzef.fi.ˈret.to   a   luːi   ri.ˈtor.na]
Little breeze, return to him

E   favellagli   per   me.
[e   fa.ˈvɛl.l.aʎ.ʎi   per   me]
And speak to him for me.

Il zeffiro

Anonymous

Vincenzo Bellini
(1801-1835)

Ven-ti-cel, che l'a - li d'o-ro vai bat-ten-do a me___ d'ap- pres - so, se ve de-sti la mia te-so - ra dim-mi, o ca - ra, dim - mi o- v'è.___

Ah! ven-ti-cel - lo,___ se ve-de-sti la mia te-so-ra, dim-mi, o

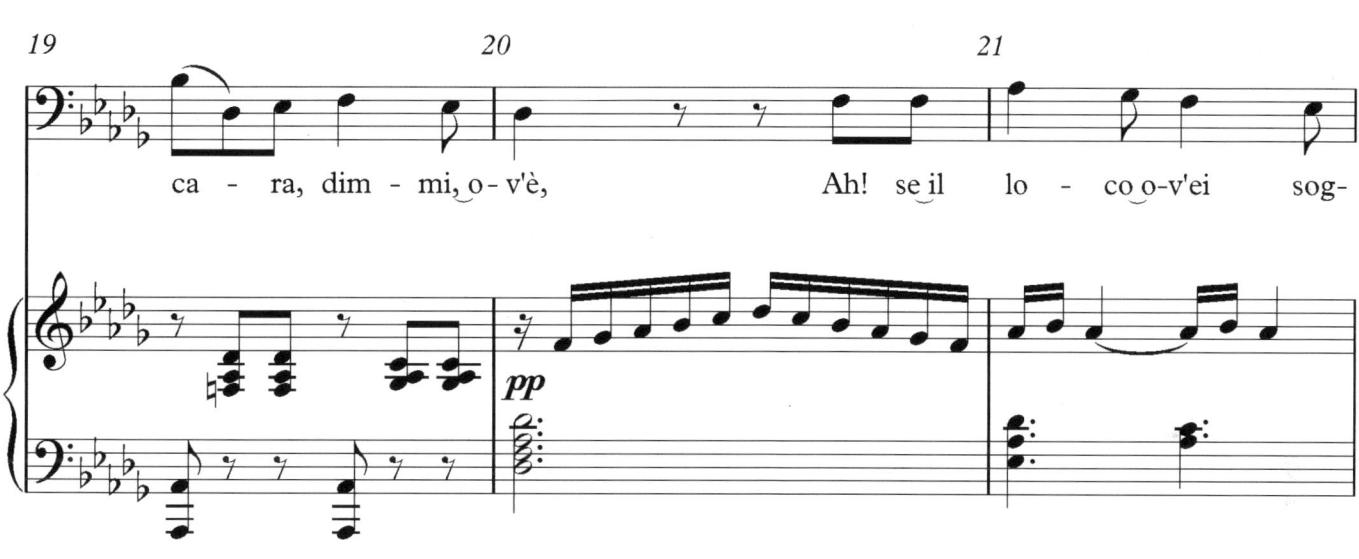

ca - ra, dim-mi, o-v'è, Ah! se il lo - co o-v'ei sog-

pp

gior - na___ pe-ne-trar non m'è__con-ces - so,___ zef-fi-ret - to, a lei__ri

tor - na__ e fa - vel - la - gli__ per me.

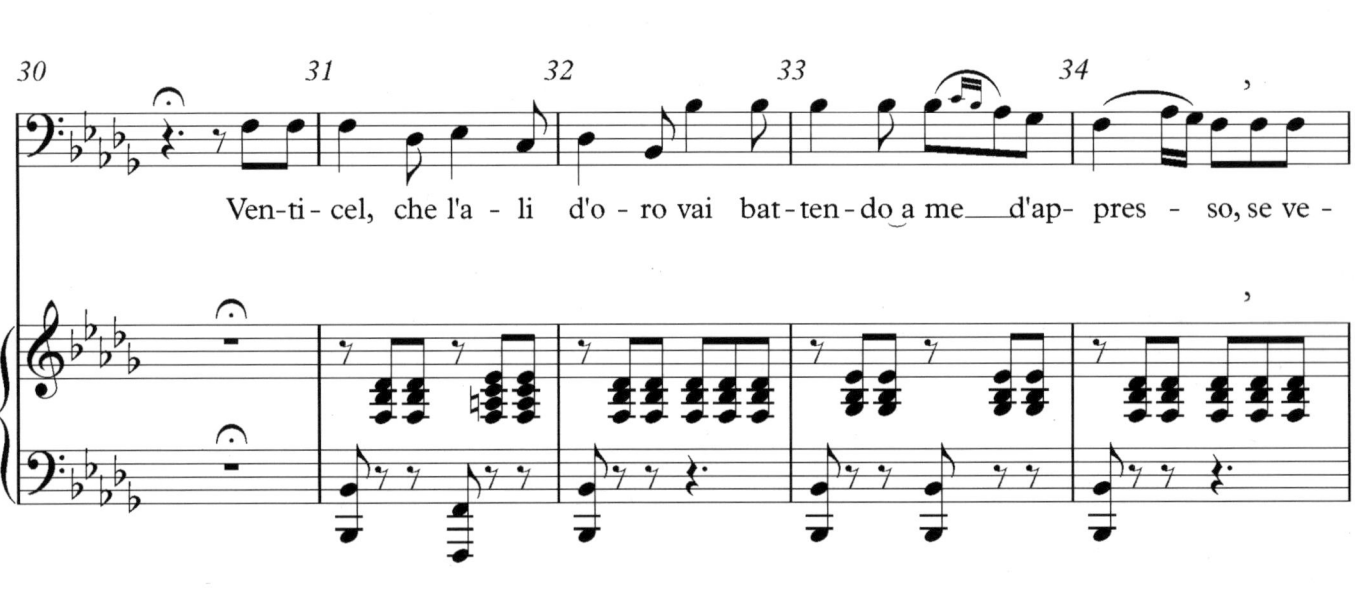

Ven-ti- cel, che l'a - li d'o - ro vai bat-ten-do a me__ d'ap- pres - so, se ve-

de - sti la mia te - so - ra, dim- mi, o ca - ra, dim-mi o-v'è. Ah! se il

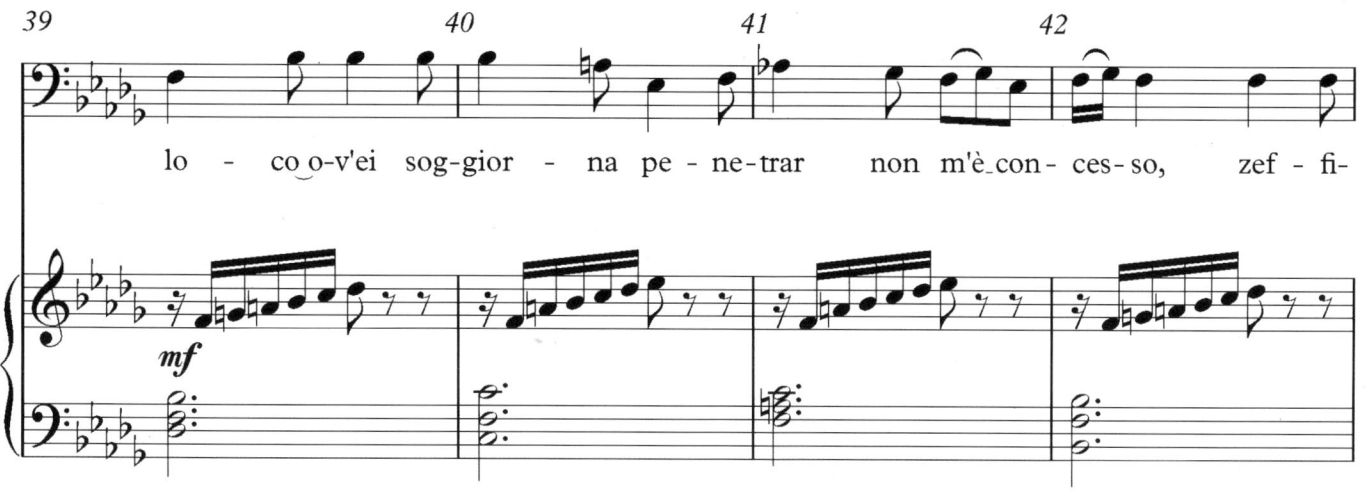

lo - co o-v'ei sog-gior - na pe - ne-trar non m'è con - ces-so, zef - fi-

ret - to, a lei ri - tor - na e fa - vel - la - gli___ per

me, e fa - vel - la - gli___ per me.

Così, Amor, mi fai languir

Italian
Alessandro Stradella

Respiration and Support

Unvoiced [s] and voiced [z] appear frequently in the text. Alternating between these two sounds, [s] and [z], hiss the text in rhythm. Next, sing the melody, alternating the sounds [zi] and [fa], as in *così* and *fai*.

Resonance

Using [ng], as in the word ring, sing the vocal melody to achieve core resonance. [Ng], when used in vocalises, should be pronounced in the dome space with an elevated soft palate and released larynx. The [ng] should not be pressed forward.

Phonation

Using the sounds [mi] and [ma], sing the melody. These sounds encourage breath flow and consistent vibration.

Registration

The alternating *piano* and *mezzo forte* dynamics will prevent a bass from singing with too much weight. Practice alternating dynamics on ascending phrases to balance registration.

Conveniently in this text, [i] frequently precedes [a] in ascending phrases. The vowel [i] is a head voice dominant vowel, which will assist in coordinating [a], which is a chest voice dominant vowel.

Diction/Articulation

Using a rounded lip position, which is essential to Italian diction, practice speaking the following words:

> *strugge*
> *fuggir*
> *così*
> *foco*

Phonetic Transcription and Translation of the Text

Così, Amor, mi fai languir,
[ko.ˈzi a.ˈmoːr mi faːi laŋ.ˈgwiːr]
Thus, Cupid, you make me languish;

non è mio ciò che desio,
[non ɛ ˈmiːo t͡ʃɔ ke de.ˈziːo]
that which I desire is not mine,

chi mi fugge seguir deggio
[ki mi ˈfud.d͡ʒe se.ˈgwiːr ˈdɛd.d͡ʒo]
I must go after the one who flees from me

e chi si strugge nel mio foco,
[e ki si ˈstrud.d͡ʒe nel ˈmiːo ˈfɔː.ko]
and the one who is consumed in love's fire for me,

nel mio foco ho da fuggir!
[nel ˈmiːo ˈfɔː.ko da fud.ˈd͡ʒir]
In love's fire for me; I must flee!

Così, Amor, mi fai penar;
[ko.ˈzi a.ˈmoːr mi faːi pe.ˈnaːr]
This is how, Cupid, you make me suffer;

non mi dai chi tanto amai,
[non mi daːi ki ˈtan.to a.ˈmaːi]
you do not give me the one I loved so much,

il mio bene scacciar deggio
[il ˈmiːo ˈbɛː.ne skat.ˈt͡ʃaːr ˈdɛd.d͡ʒo]
I must chase my beloved away

e mi conviene chi non amo,
[e mi kon.ˈvjɛː.ne ki non ˈaː.mo]
and be destined to love the one

chi non amo pur amar.
[ki non ˈaː.mo puːr a.ˈmaːr]
I do not love.

Così, Amor, mi fai languir

Alessandro Stradella
(1639-1682)

Co - sì, a - mor, mi fai lan - guir, mi fai lan - guir, co - sì a - mor, mi fai lan -
Co - sì, a - mor, mi fai pe - nar, mi fai pe - nar, co - sì, a - mor, mi fai pe -

guir, mi fai lan - guir, non è mi - o ciò che de - si - o, chi mi fug - ge se - guir
nar, mi fai pe - nar, non mi dai chi tan - to a - ma - i, il mio be - ne scac - ciar

deg - gio e chi si strug - ge nel mio fo - co, nel mio fo - co, ho da fug
deg - gio e mi con vie - ne chi non a - mo, chi non a - mo pur a -

10

2

11

Mädchen mit dem roten Mündchen

German
Robert Franz

Respiration and Support

1. Inhale for two measures through an imaginary straw, and then exhale for two measures through the same imaginary straw.
2. Take another breath, and then exhale.
3. Inhale slowly and easily while form the words: *Mädchen mit dem roten Mündchen*.
4. Immediately speak this same text while exhaling, using the same amount of air as in step 3.

Resonance

Intone the text, lingering on [m], which appears frequently.

[ˈmmmɛt.çən   mmmɪt   deːmmm   ˈroː.tən   ˈmmmʏnt.çən]

Next, intone the text on one pitch, maintaining the sensations experienced.

Continue this pattern as the melody is sung.

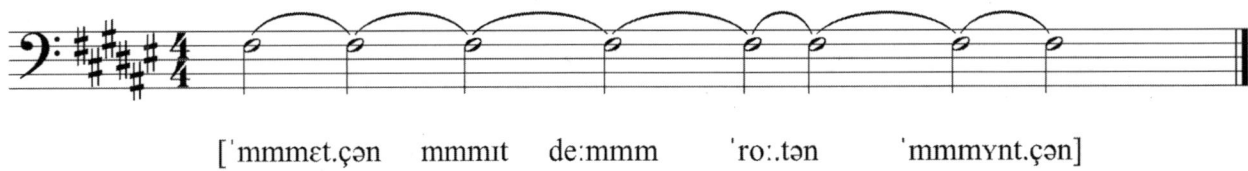

[ˈmmmɛt.çən   mmmɪt   deːmmm   ˈroː.tən   ˈmmmʏnt.çən]

Phonation

Practice the melody on [v] with easy, consistent vibration. Next, sing [v] before the vowels in the text.

[v]
[vɛ və vɪ ve   vo   və   vʏ   və   vɪ ve vɔːʏ   vaːe   vʏ vʊ vaːɐ]

Registration
Using a lip trill/flutter, begin quietly, and increase the dynamic level when singing this descending melody. Next, practice the < > (*crescendo/decresendo*) using a lip trill to mimic the dynamics of the piece.

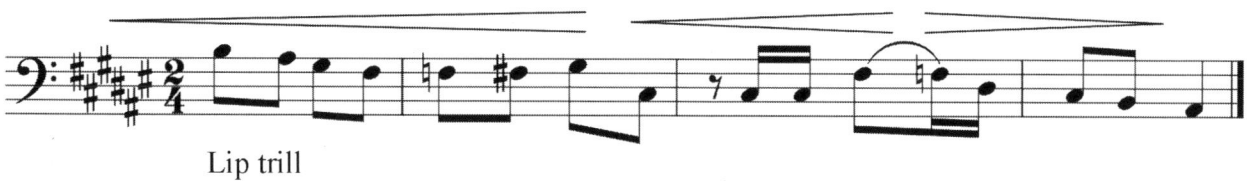

Lip trill

Diction/Articulation
Many of the sounds will need clarification. Please refer to the I.P.A. guide found in the front of this book.

To address the syllabic nature of this piece, and to encourage legato articulation, practice the text on one pitch in rhythm before adding the melody.

Mäd- chen mit dem ro - ten Münd- chen, mit den Äug - lein süß und klar

Notice that many German words end with a *schwa* sound: [ə]. This is a unique speech sound in German that requires practice. Many American singers incorrectly use the wrong sounds. This was Lindsey Christiansen's[1] explanation of *Schwa*:

> After bright vowels, shaded toward [ɛ]: liebe, schwebe
> After rounded vowels, shaded toward rounded [ə]: möchte, rufe
> When these sounds appear at the end of a word: en, el, es, et, er, shaded toward darker [ə]: Himmel, Mutter

---

[1] Professor Christiansen was a prominent singing teacher who spent most of her career teaching at Westminster Choir College

Phonetic Transcription and Translation of the Text

Mädchen mit dem roten Mündchen,
[ˈmɛt.çən mɪt deːm ˈroː.tən ˈmʏnt.çən]
Maiden with your little red mouth,

mit den Äuglein süß und klar,
[mɪt deːn̥ ˈʔɔːɤk.laːen zyːs ʔʊnt klaːɐ̯]
with your little eyes so sweet and clear,

Du mein liebes, (süßes) kleines Mädchen,
[duː maːen ˈliː.bəs (ˈzyː.səs) ˈklaːe.nəs ˈmɛt.çən]
you, my dearest, (sweetest) little maiden,

deiner denk' ich immerdar.
[ˈdaːe.nɐ dɛŋk ʔɪç ˈʔɪ.mɐ.daːɐ̯]
I will think about you always.

Lang ist heut der Winterabend,
[laŋ ʔɪst hɔːʏt deːɐ̯ ˈvɪn.tɐ.ˌʔaː.bənt]
Long is this winter evening,

und ich möchte bei dir sein,
[ʔʊnt ʔɪç ˈmœç.tə baːe diːɐ̯ zaːen]
and I want to be with you,

bei dir sitzen, mit (bei) dir schwatzen,
[baːe diːɐ̯ ˈzɪ.tsən mɪt (baːe) diːɐ̯ ˈʃva.tsən]
sitting with you, and chatting with you,

im vertrauten Kämmerlein.
[ʔɪm fɛɐ̯.ˈtraːu.tən ˈkɛ.mɐ.laːen]
in a cozy little room.

An die Lippen wollt' ich pressen
[ʔan diː ˈlɪ.pən vɔlt ʔɪç ˈprɛ.sən]
I would press to my lips

deine kleine weiße Hand,
[ˈdaːe.nə ˈklaːe.nə ˈvaːe.sə hant]
your small white hand,

und mit Tränen sie benetzen,
[ʔʊnt mɪt ˈtrɛː.nən ziː bə.ˈnɛ.tsən]
and wet with my tears,

deine kleine, weiße Hand.
[ˈdaːe.nə ˈklaːe.nə ˈvaːe.sə hant]
your small white hand.

Mädchen mit dem roten Mündchen

Op. 5 N. 5

Heinrich Heine

Robert Franz
(1815-1892)

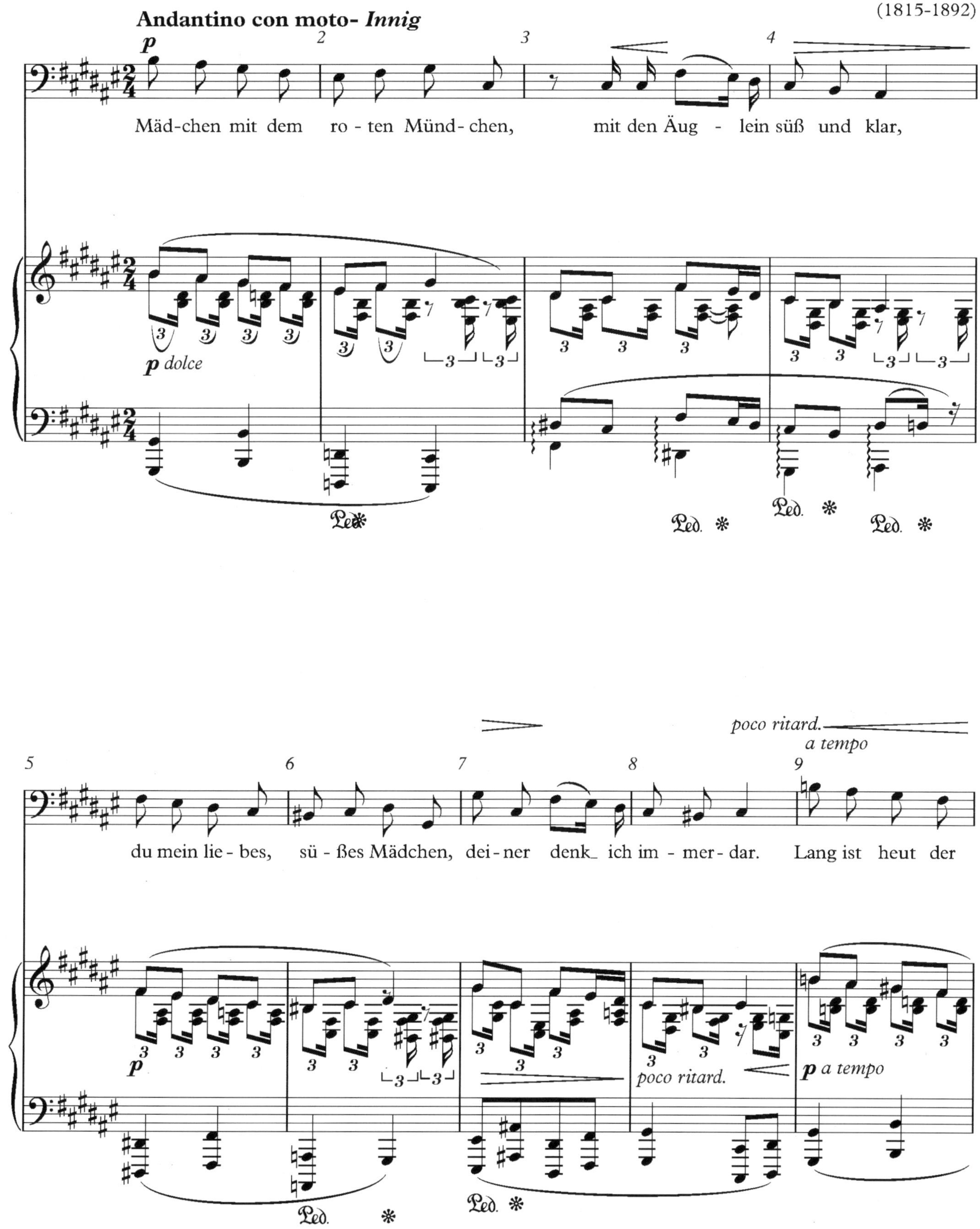

Andantino con moto- *Innig*

Mäd-chen mit dem ro-ten Münd-chen, mit den Äug - lein süß und klar,

du mein lie-bes, sü - ßes Mädchen, dei-ner denk ich im - mer-dar. Lang ist heut der

Win - ter - a - bend und ich möch - te bei dir sein, bei dir sit - zen,

mit dir schwat - zen im ver - trau - ten

Käm - mer - lein. An die Lip - pen wollt ich pres - sen

riten.

mf Mit Wärme

Meeresleuchten

German
Carl Loewe

Respiration and Support

The eighth-note pattern found frequently throughout this piece assists in flexible breathing. Use the rhythm of vocal line found in measures 6-7, and bounce on the vowels (elongated staccato) in the pattern of the vocal line. Rearticulating the vowel should feel like laughing in this exercise.

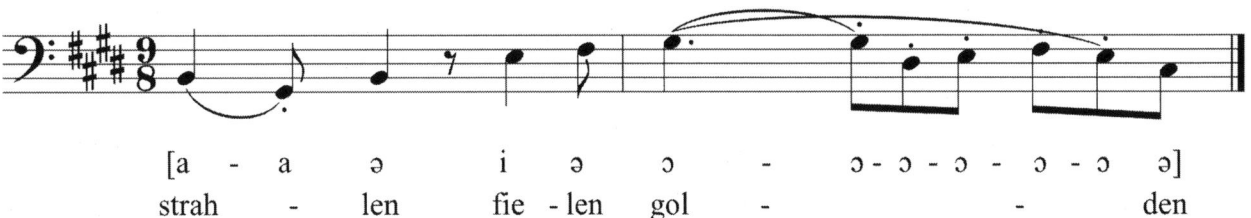

Resonance

To balance resonance in the bass voice, it is important to alternate forward and back vowels in vocalises. This text includes many examples of this: i.e. *die Wogen*. Alternate between these vowels to neutralize the position of the larynx for consistent resonance.

Phonation

The many fricatives in this text provide opportunities to maintain breath flow and consistent vocal fold vibration.

Sonnenstrahlen

ˈzzzɔ.nən. ʃʃʃtraː.lən

Feierstund'

ˈfffaːe.ɐ. ʃʃʃtʊnt

funkensprüh'nde

ˈfffʊŋ.kən. ʃʃʃpryː.n.də

Registration

Use the following vocal exercises with vowels chosen from the song to assist with bass registration.

Diction/Articulation

Muddy vocal quality commonly is found in young basses, so it is important that they sing with clear, intelligible vowels in the low range. This piece gives an opportunity to address this issue as it descends to low G-sharp^2, F#-sharp^2, and E^2. Extra coloring of the voice in this range is unnecessary.

Practice 5 note scales, beginning in the middle of the voice, maintaining the pure vowel when descending.

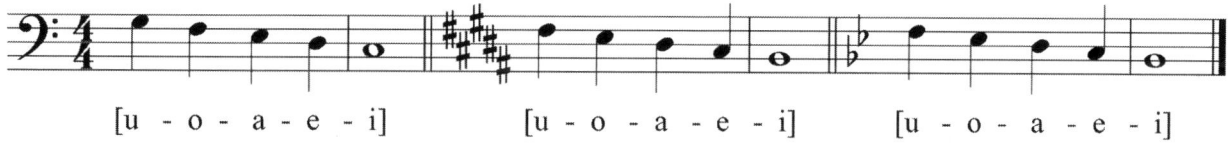

Phonetic Transcription and Translation of the Text

Wieviel Sonnenstrahlen fielen goldenschwer,
[ˈviː.fiːl ˈzɔ.nən.ʃtraː.lən ˈfiː.lən ˈgɔl.dən.ʃveːɐ̯]
Many heavy gold sunbeams fell,

Fielen feurig glühend in des ew'ge Meer!
[ˈfiː.lən ˈfɔːʏ.rɪç ˈglyː.ənt ʔɪn dɛs ˈʔevːgə meːɐ̯]
fell glowing like fire into the eternal sea!

Und die Woge sog sie tief in sich hinab,
[ʔʊnt diː ˈvoː.gə zoːk ziː tiːf ʔɪn zɪç hɪn.ˈap]
And the waves drew them down, deep within,

Und die Woge ward ihr wild lebendig Grab.
[ʔʊnt diː ˈvoː.gə vart ʔiːɐ̯ vɪlt le.ˈbɛn.dɪç graːp]
and the waves became their living tomb.

Nur in stiller Nächte heilger Feierstund'
[nuːɐ̯ ʔɪn ˈʃtɪːlɐ ˈnɛçːtə ˈhaːelːgɐ ˈfaːe.ɐ̯.ˌʃtʊnt]
Only in the peaceful hour of the quiet night

Sprühen diese Strahlen aus des Meeres Grund.
[ˈʃpryː.ən ˈdiː.zə ˈʃtraː.lən ʔaːus dɛs ˈmeː.rəs grʊnt]
are these rays released from the sea's depths.

Leuchtend roll'n die Wogen durch die dunkle Nacht
[ˈlɔːʏç.tənt rɔln diː ˈvoː.gən dʊrç diː ˈdʊŋk.lə naxt]
Shining, the waves roll through the dark night

Wunderbar durchglüht sie funkensprüh'nde Pracht
[ˈvʊn.dɐ.baːɐ̯ dʊrç.ˈglyːt ziː ˈfʊŋ.kən.ˌʃpryːn.də praxt]
shimmering wondrously with glittering splendor.

Meeresleuchten

from *Liederkranz für die Bassstimme*

Op. 145 N.1

Carl Seibel

Carl Loewe
(1796-1869)

1.Wie viel Son - - nen ler
2.Nun in stil - - ler

strah - len fie - len gol - - den schwer, fie - len
Näch - te heil' - ger Fei - - er-stund sprü-hen

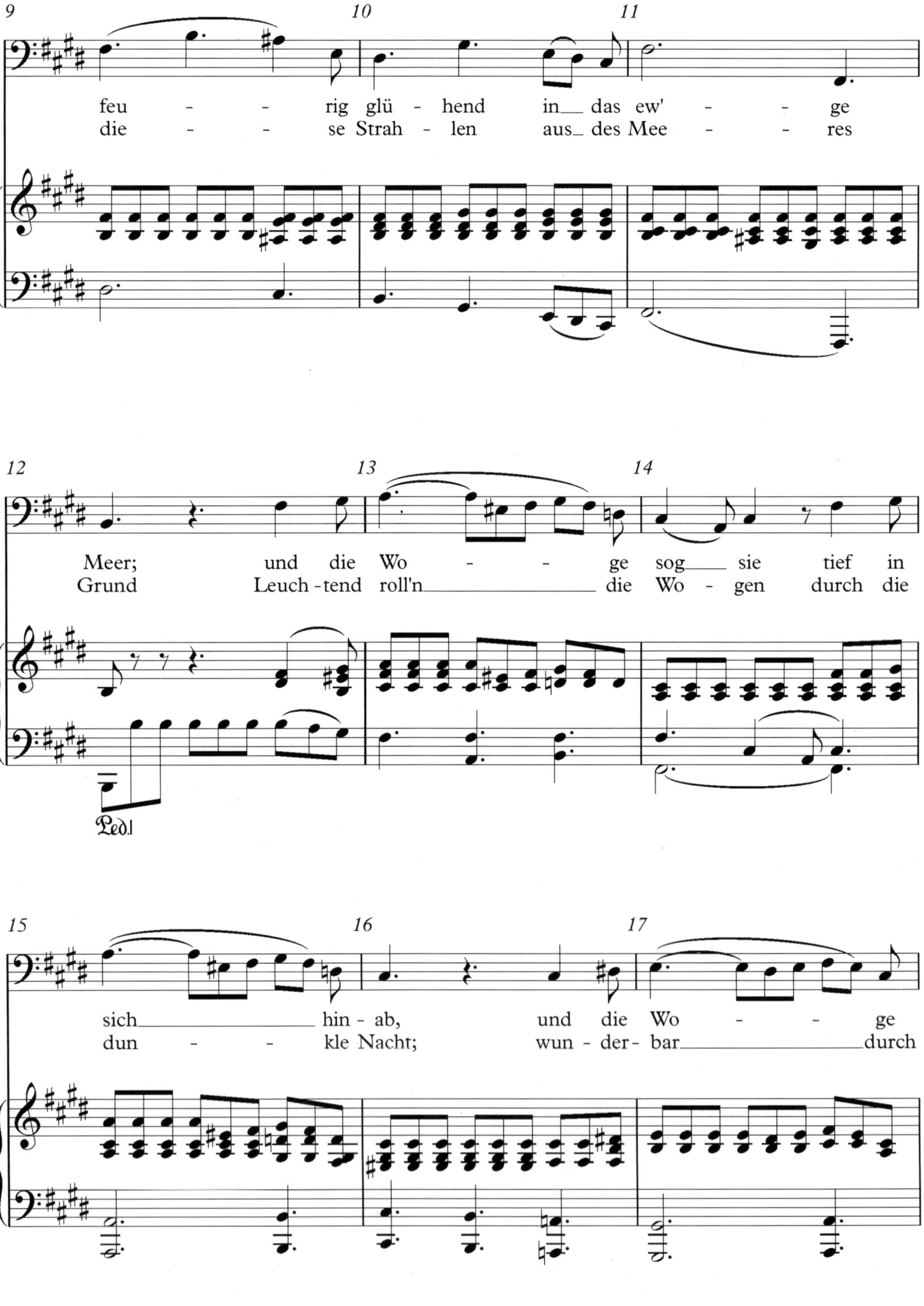

feu - - rig glü - hend in das ew' - ge
die - - se Strah - len aus des Mee - - res

Meer; und die Wo - - ge sog sie tief in
Grund Leuch - tend roll'n die Wo - gen durch die

Ped.

sich hin - ab, und die Wo - ge
dun - - kle Nacht; wun - der - bar durch

22

ward _____ ihr wild le - ben - - dig
glüht _____ sie funk - en -sprüh'n - de

Grab.
Pracht.

D.S. 𝄋

Colette

French
Cécile Chaminade

Respiration and Support
Because this is a syllabic song, it is necessary to impart the idea that legato is caused by breath that does not stop and start. Using a cup with a very small amount of water and a straw, the singer should blow bubbles while vocalizing the melody, which will allow him to see the result of consistent and energized breath flow. Transition to the text and maintain the same feeling of even, legato breath.

Resonance
This text contains [d] consonants, *voiced* lingua-alveolar stop plosives, and [t] consonants, *voiceless* lingua-alveolar stop plosives. These consonants can add significantly to desirable resonance if produced correctly, without the jaw. Speak the following:

[ta ta ta ta ta]
[da da da da da]
[tada tada tada tada tada]

Phonation
This song contains larger intervals. To encourage legato while singing them, sing the following exercise through a straw, and then on an [u]. This vocalise prepares the singer for large intervallic leaps.

Registration
In the bass voice, the first *passaggio* is around A-flat[3]. To invite more head voice, the soft palate must be elevated and the larynx released so that the vocal folds can stretch. A snort or sniff can help to achieve this. While singing the melody on vowels from the text, instruct him to use a snort or sniff at the rests, which will help to create awareness of the soft palate and to release the larynx.

Diction/Articulation
Ask the singer to whisper the text, noticing that the jaw is relaxed and the tongue is doing its job by articulating consonants with ease. Add voice, and watch in the mirror. The jaw and tongue should be independent and free.

Phonetic Transcription and Translation of the Text

Avril a parlé, Colette est rêveuse
[a.vʀi.‿la par.le ko.lɛ.‿ tɛ ʀɛ.vøz]
April has spoken, Colette is dreaming

Elle a délaissé les jeux d'autrefois!
[ɛ.‿la. de.lɛ.se le.‿ʒø do.tʀə.fwa]
She has left her old games!

Mais quand des oiseaux la troupe amoureuse
[mɛ kɑ̃ de.‿zwa.zo la tru.‿pa.mu.ʀø.zə]
But when the flock of enamored birds

Chante du printemps les divins exploits,
[ʃɑ̃.tə dy pʀɛ̃.tɑ̃ le di.vɛ̃.‿zeks.plwa]
sings of spring's divine exploits

Elle écoute, heureuse,
[ɛ. ‿le.ku. ‿tø.ʀø.zə]
she listens, happy

Au fond des grands bois!
[o fõ dɛ gʀɑ̃ bwa]
in the depths of the great wood!

Tout parle à son coeur, rumeurs bocagères,
[tu par.‿la sõ kœr ʀy.mør bɔ.ka.ʒɛ.ʀə]
Everything speaks to her heart, murmurs of the woodland,

Parfums caressants |ou rayons joyeux!
[par.fœ̃ ka.ʀɛ.sɑ̃ o ʀɛ.jõ ʒwa.jø]
caressing fragrances and joyful rays!

Vénus ou Phoebé, d'amour messagère,
[ve.ny u fœ.be da.mur mɛ.sa.ʒɛ.ʀə]
Venus and Phoebe, messengers of love,

Lui semblent des yeux fixés sur ses yeux,
[lɥi sɑ̃.blə de.‿zjø fi.kse syr se.‿zjø]
seem to have their starry gaze fixed on her eyes,

Les brises légères
[lɛ bʀi.zə le.ʒɛ.ʀə]
the light breezes,

Un soupir des cieux!
[œ̃ su.pir de.‿sjø]
are the sighs of heaven!

Le gentil Colin, depuis sa naissance,
[lə ʒɑ̃.ti kɔ.lɛ̃ də.pɥi sa nɛ.sɑ̃.sə]
Sweet Colin, since his birth,

Avait ses baisers d'enfant chaque jour;
[a.vɛ se be.ze dɑ̃.fɑ̃ ʃa.kə ʒuɾ]
has had her innocent kisses each day;

Tous deux ignoraient l'étrange puissance
[tu dø.‿zi.ɲɔ.ɾɛ le.tɾɑ̃.ʒə pɥi.sɑ̃.sə]
the two unaware of the strange power

D'un baiser qu'on donne et prend tour à tour!
[dœ̃ be.ze kɔ̃ dɔ.‿ne pɾɑ̃ tu.‿ɾa tuɾ]
of a kiss given and taken in its turn!

Mais leur innocence
[mɛ lø.‿ɾi.nɔ.sɑ̃.sə]
Yet their innocence

Leur apprit l'amour!
[lø.‿ɾa.pɾi la.muɾ]
taught them of love!

Colin, |un matin, la voyant paraître,
[kɔ.lɛ̃ œ̃ ma.tɛ̃ la vwa.jɑ̃ pa.ɾɛ.tɾə]
Colin, one morning, seeing her appear,

Lui voulut |au front ses lèvres poser,
[lɥi vuly o fɾɔ̃ sɛ lɛ.vɾə po.ze]
wanted to press his lips to her brow,

Elle eut un caprice où l'amour put naître
[ɛ.‿lø.‿tœ̃ ka.pɾi.sə u la.muɾ py nɛ.tɾə]
and on a whim, its source of love,

Et se fit un jeu de s'y refuser,
[e sə fi.‿tœ̃ ʒø də si ɾe.fy.ze]
she made a game of refusing him,

Lors il put connaître
[lɔɾ.‿zil py kɔ.nɛ.tɾɛ]
so that he could know

Le prix d'un baiser.
[lə pɾi dœ̃ be.ze]
the price of a kiss.

Page intentionally left blank to facilitate page turns

Colette

P. Barbier

Cécile Chaminade
(1857-1944)

Allegro

A-vril a par-lé, Co-let-te est rê-veu -

se! El-le a dé lais-sé les jeux d'au-tre-fois! Mais quand des oi - seaux la

troupe a-mon- reu - se Chan-te du prin-temps les di - vins ex - ploits,

El le é-cou-te, heu-reu - se, Au fond des grands bois! Tout par-le á son coeur,

ru-meurs bo-ca-gè - res, Par-fums ca-res-sants ou ray - ons joy - eux!

de-puis sa nais-san - ce, A - vait ses bai-sers d'en - fant cha-que jour;

Tous deux i-gno-raient l'é-tran-ge puis-san - ce D'un bai-ser qu'on donne et

prend tour à tour! Mais leur in - no-cen - ce Leur ap-prit l'a-mour!

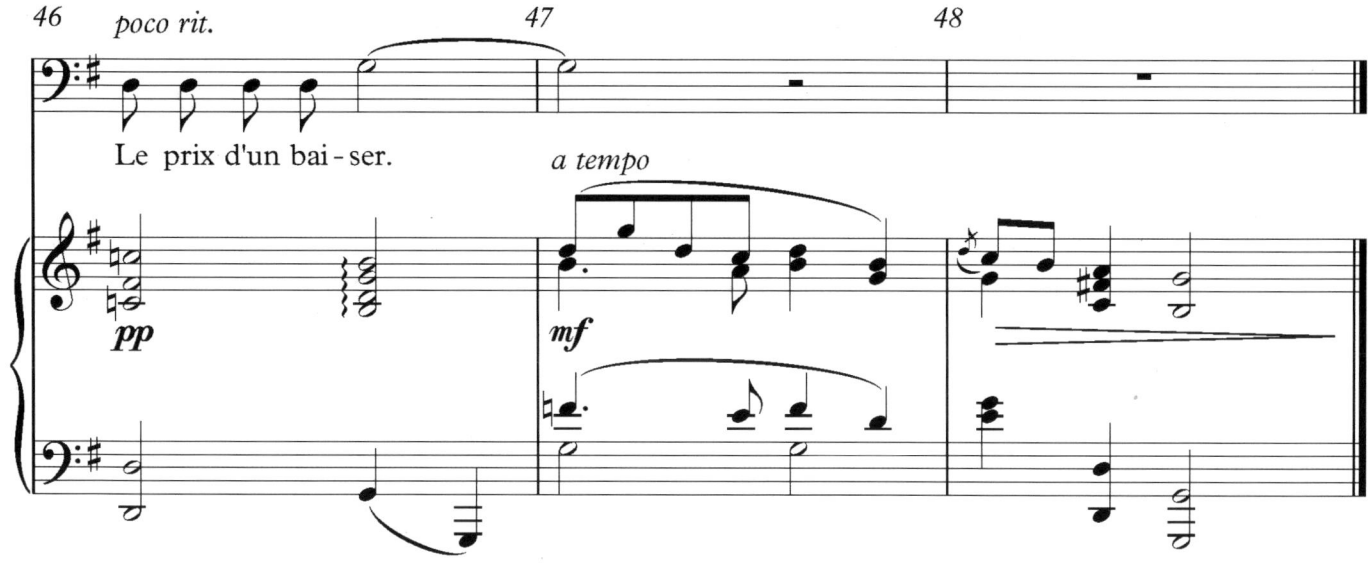

Le prix d'un bai - ser.

Trois poèmes d'amour

French
Érik Satie

Respiration and Support

Using the concept of *martellato* (pulsed and detached legato) speak the following:

1. Staccato- [a̤ a a a a a a]
2. Pulsed- [a a a a a a a]
3. Detached and legato- [a a a a a a a]
4. Pulse the text of this song:

Ne	suis	que	grain	de	sable...
[nə	sɥi	kə	gɾɛ̃	də	sab.lə]...

Resonance

To help students to become familiar with resonant and distinct French sounds, sing and alternate the following French sounds, maintaining clarity in each.

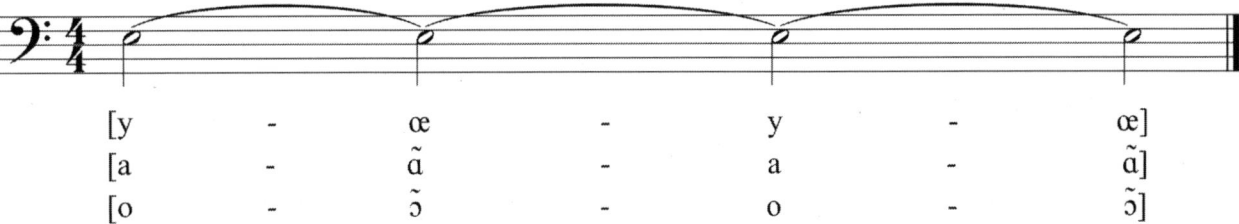

Phonation

To encourage consistent vibrancy and space, imitate an owl, "Who" [huuu]. Next, speak the words while maintaining the quality of the owl, using inflection.

Registration

This piece affords ample opportunities to achieve balanced registration in the low range. It is the tendency of basses to over-darken the sound by depressing the larynx. To neutralize the position, sing the melody, alternating the sounds [gʌg] and [ne].

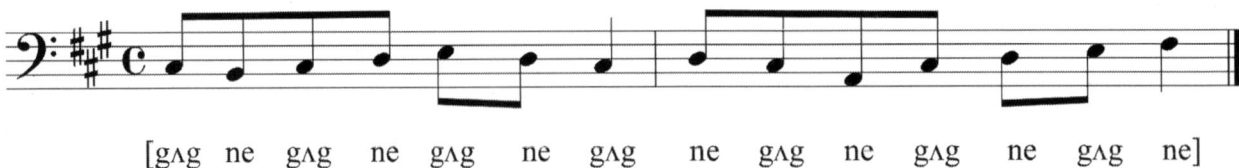

Diction/Articulation

In French, it is necessary to minimize syllabic stress. Sing the text on a single pitch in the middle voice, maintaining a consistent dynamic level.

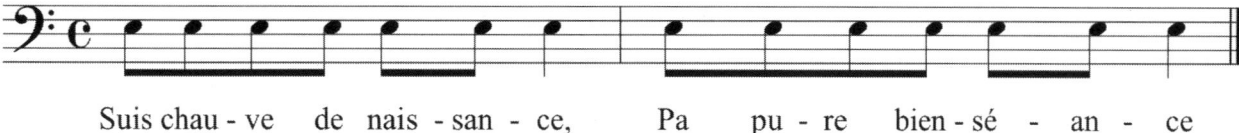

Suis chau - ve de nais - san - ce, Pa pu - re bien - sé - an - ce

Phonetic Transcription and Translation of the Text

N. 1

Ne   suis   que   grain   de   sable,
[nə   sɥi   kə   grɛ̃   də   sab.lə]
I am only a grain of sand

Toujours   frais et   t'aimable,
[tu.ʒur   frɛ‿ze   tɛ.ma.blə]
Always fresh and sweet to you,

Qui   boit,   qui   rit,   qui   chante
[ki   bwa   ki   ri   ki   ʃɑ̃.tə]
Which drinks, and laughs, and sings

Pour   plaire à   son amante.
[pur   plɛ‿ra   sɔ̃‿na.mɑ̃.tə]
All to please his lover.

Tout   doux,   ma   chère   belle
[tu   du   ma   ʃɛ.rə   bɛ.lə]
Softly now, my beautiful dear

Aimez   votre   amant   frêle;
[ɛ.me   vɔ‿tra.mɑ̃   frɛ.lə]
Love your little lover;

Il   n'est   que grain   de   sable,
[il   nɛ   kə   grɛ̃   də   sab.lə]
It is only a grain of sand,

Toujours frais et   t'aimable.
[tu.ʒur   frɛ‿ze   tɛ.ma.blə]
Always fresh and sweet to you.

N. 2

Suis   chauve   de   naissance,
[sɥi   ʃo.və   də   nɛ.sɑ̃.sə]
I have been bald since birth,

Par   pure   bienséance
[par   py.rə   bjɛ̃.se.ɑ̃.sə]
For propriety's sake

Je   n'ai   plus   confiance
[ʒə   nɛ   ply   kɔ̃.fjɑ̃.sə]
I no longer rely

En   ma   jeune   vaillance.
[ɑ̃   ma   ʒø.nə   va.jɑ̃.sə]
On my youthful boldness.

Pourquoi   cette   arrogance.
[pur.kwa   sɛ‿ta.rɔ.gɑ̃.sə]
Why this arrogance,

De   la   si   belle Hortense?
[də   la   si   bɛ.lɔr.tɑ̃.sə]
From the beautify Hortense?

Très   chauve   de   naissance,
[trɛ   ʃo.və   də   nɛ.sɑ̃.sə]
Completely bald since birth,

Le   suis   par   bienséance.
[lə   sɥi   par   bjɛ̃.se.ɑ̃.sə]
I embody propriety.

N. 3

Ta parure est secrète,
[ta pa.ry.‿ ɾɛ se.kɾɛ.tə]
Your adornment is secret,

Ô douce luronnette.
[o du.sə ly.ɾɔ.nɛ.tə]
O sweet and small one.

Ma belle guillerette
[ma bɛ.lə gi.jə.ɾɛ.tə]
My beautiful and cheerful one,

Fume la cigarette
[fy.mə la si.ga.ɾɛ.tə]
Smokes the cigarette

Ferai - je sa conquête,
[fə.ɾe ʒə sa kɔ̃.kɛ.tə]
Will I become its conquest,

Que je voudrais complète?
[kə ʒə vu.dɾɛ kɔ̃.plɛ.tə]
Because I want to finish it?

Ta parure est secrète,
[ta pa.ry.‿ɾɛ se.kɾɛ.tə]
Your adornment is secret

Ô douce luronnette.
[o du.sə ly.ɾɔ.nɛ.tə]
Oh little sweet one.

Trois poèmes d'amour
N. 1

Erik Satie (1866-1925)

Ne suis que grain de sa-ble, Tou-jours frais et t'ai-ma-ble. Qui boit, qui rit, qui chan-te

Pour plaire à son a-man-te. Tout doux, ma chè-re bel-le Ai-mez vo-tre a-mant frêle:

Il n'est que grain de sa - ble, Tou -jours frais et t'aim - a - ble.

Spring Sorrow

English
John Ireland

Respiration and Support

Practice the irregular rhythmic patterns in this song with planned breaths in place before adding pitches. Mark your score and practice these catch breaths.

Resonance

The British vowel sounds in a young bass can become too dark because of a tendency to depress the back of the tongue. Practice sequences of the following vowel pattern, with awareness of high sensations of resonance: [a ɔ ə].

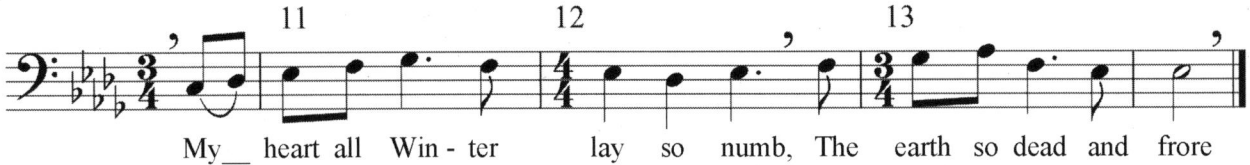

My__ heart all Win - ter   lay   so   numb,   The   earth   so   dead   and   frore

Practice the melody on this pattern: [za zɔ zə].

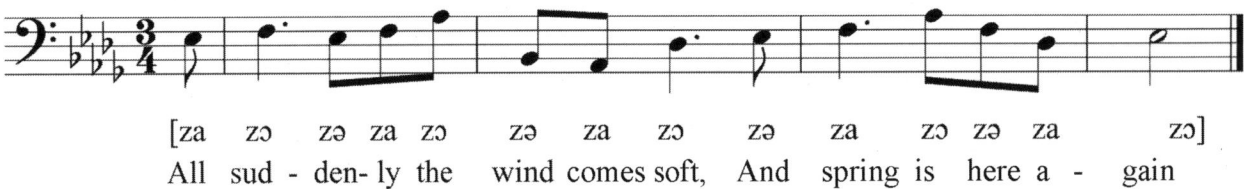

[za   zɔ   zə   za   zɔ   zə   za   zɔ   zə   za   zɔ   zə   za   zɔ]
All   sud - den- ly   the   wind   comes soft,   And   spring   is   here   a -   gain

Phonation

Use "blenders" to assist in consistent resonance. Use [z], the voiced s, at the ends of words to connect to the following word:

Quickens with / Quickenz‿with
Buds of / Budz‿of
Winter's broken / Winter'z‿broken

Registration

A pattern of four eighth-notes always precedes the highest pitch in this song. Practice this excerpt from the piece with dotted rhythms to maintain a flexible laryngeal position, to avoid carrying too much weight to the top, and to assist in aligning registration. Sing this first on [o i o i o i], then reverse to [i o i o i o], then sing the text.

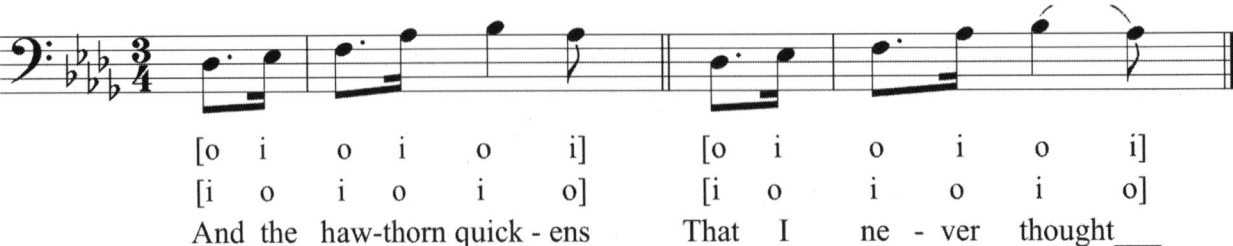

[o   i   o   i   o   i]   [o   i   o   i   o   i]
[i   o   i   o   i   o]   [i   o   i   o   i   o]
And   the   haw-thorn quick - ens   That   I   ne - ver   thought___

Diction/Articulation

John Ireland is a British composer, therefore British-received diction should be addressed. Here are some examples of transcribed words to assist:

Here- [hiɚ]
Again- [əgeɪn]
Hawthorn- [hɔ:θɔ:n] (the r is not pronounced)
Green- [gɾin] (the r is flipped)

N.B. The Oxford British Dictionary online is helpful and convenient!

Phonetic Transcription of the Text

All   suddenly   the   wind   comes   soft,
[ɔl   'sʌ.dən.li   ðʌ   wɪnd   kʌmz   sɔft]

And   Spring   is   here   again;
[ænd   spɹɪŋ   ɪz   hɪɹ̊   ə'.gɛn]

And   the   hawthorn   quickens   with   buds   of   green,
[ænd   ðʌ   'hɔ.θɔɹ̊n   'kwɪ.kənz   wɪθ   bʌdz   ʌv   gɹin]

And   my   heart   with   buds   of   pain.
[ænd   ma:ɪ   hɑɹ̊t   wɪθ   bʌdz   ʌv   pe:ɪn]

My   heart   all   Winter   lay   so   numb,
[ma:ɪ   hɑɹ̊t   ɔl   'wɪn.tɐ   le:ɪ   so:ʊ   nʌm]

The   earth   so   dead   and   frore,
[ði   ɜθ   so:ʊ   dɛd   ænd   fɹɔɹ̊]

That   I   never   thought   the   Spring   would   come,
[ðæt   a:ɪ   'nɛ.vɐ   θa:ʊt   ðʌ   spɹɪŋ   wʊd   kʌm]

Or   my   heart   wake   anymore.
[ɔɹ̊   ma:ɪ   hɑɹ̊t   we:ɪk   ɛ.ni.'mɔɹ̊]

But   Winter's   broken   and   earth   has   woken,
[bʌt   'wɪn.tɐz   'bɹo:ʊk.ən   ænd   ɜθ   hæz   'wo:ʊk.ən]

And   the   small   birds   cry   again;
[ænd   ðʌ   smɔl   bɜdz   cɹa:ɪ   ə.'gɛn]

And   the   hawthorn   hedge   puts   forth   its   buds
[ænd   ðʌ   'hɔ.θɔɹ̊n   hɛdʒ͡   pʊts   fɔɹ̊θ   ɪts   bʌdz]

And   my   heart   puts   forth   its   pain.
[ænd   ma:ɪ   hɑɹ̊t   pʊts   fɔɹ̊θ   ɪts   pe:ɪn]

Spring Sorrow

Rupert Brooke

John Ireland
(1879-1962)

All sud - den - ly the wind comes soft, And Spring is here a - gain; And the haw-thorn quick - ens with buds of green, And my heart with buds of

pain. My__ heart all Win - ter lay so numb, The

earth so dead and frore, That I nev - er thought__ the

Spring would come, Or my heart wake a - ny - more. But

Win-ter's bro - ken and earth has wok - en, And the small birds cry a-

gain; And the haw-thorn hedge__ puts forth its buds And my

heart puts forth its pain.__

Drake's Drum

English
Charles Villiers Stanford

Respiration and Support

Because of the march tempo, there may be a tendency to stop or stiffen the breath flow. Speak a pulsed [s] to the rhythm of the song to create flexibility in the muscles of breathing.

Resonance

Paying close attention to the frequently changing dotted rhythm patterns of this song, speak the text maintaining a smooth transition from syllable to syllable.

Slung a-tween the round shot in Nombre Dios Bay,
And dreaming all the time of Plymouth Hoe.

Next, sing this, maintaining the legato found in the spoken text.

Phonation

There may be a tendency in this song to sing straight tone eighth notes (without vibrato). To avoid this, practice singing at a very slow tempo, maintaining a vibrant tone throughout all of the note values, which will help to create correct muscle memory.

Sing this example very slowly, maintaining vibrancy throughout the eighth-notes.

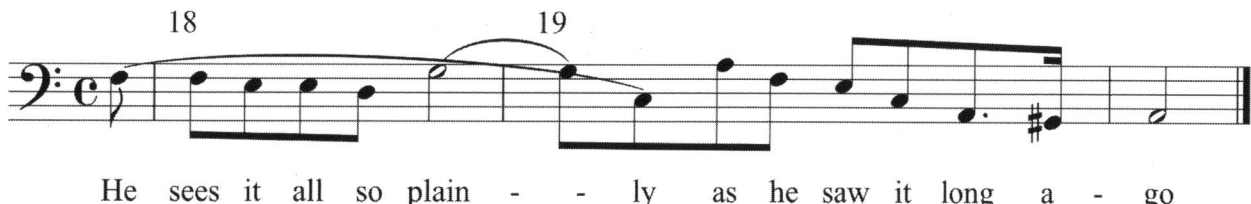

Registration
Because of the characterization of this piece, there will be a tendency to sing with too much vocal weight. It is particularly important in the bass voice to be sure that there is adequate head register participation. Practice speaking the piece using an exaggerated yawn, a hoot-y [u] and/or an imitation of Yogi Bear to release the larynx and encourage more head voice.

Diction/Articulation
It is necessary to teach British-received diction in this piece. Some of the important components are:

The lessening of "r" colorations.
The substitution of [ɑ] for the American [æ].
Pronouncing [ju] rather than [u]- i.e. ['mju zɪk]
The [ʍ], "wh", sound.

Phonetic Transcription of the Text

Drake,	he's	in	his	hammock	and	a	thousand	miles	away
[dɹeːɪk	hiz	ɪn	hɪz	'hæ.mək	ænd	ʌ	'θaːʊ.zənd	maːɪlz	ə'.weːɪ]

(Captain,	art	though	sleeping	there	below?)
['kæp.tən	ɑɐt	ðaːʊ	'slip.ɪŋ	ðɛɐ̯	bə.'loːʊ]

Slung	atween	the	round	shot	in	Nombre	Dios	Bay,
[slʊŋ	ə.'twin	ðʌ	ɾaːʊnd	ʃɑt	ɪn	'nɔm.bɾɛ	'di.ɔz	beːɪ]

And	dreaming	all	the	time	of	Plymouth	Hoe.
[ænd	'dɹim.ɪŋ	ɑl	ðʌ	taːɪm	ʌv	'plɪ.məθ	hoːʊ]

Yonder	lumes	the	island	yonder	lie	the	ships,
['jɑn.dɐ̯	lumz	ði	'aːɪ.lənd	'jɑn.dɐ̯	laːɪ	ðʌ	ʃɪps]

With	sailor	lads	a-dancing	heel -	an' -	toe
[wɪð	'seːɪ.lɐ̯	lædz	ə.'dæns.ɪŋ	hil	æn -	toːʊ]

And	the	shore-lights	flashing	and	the	night-tide	dashing,
[ænd	ðʌ	'ʃɔɐ̯.laːɪts	'flæʃ.ɪŋ	ænd	ðʌ	'naːɪ.taːɪd	'dæʃ.ɪŋ]

He	sees	it	all	so	plainly	as	he	saw	it	long	ago.
[hi	siz	ɪt	ɔl	soːʊ	'pleːɪn.li	æz	hi	sɔ	ɪt	lɔŋ	ə.'goːʊ]

Drake	he	was	a	Devon	man,	and	ruled	the	Devon	seas,
[dɹeːɪk	hi	wæz	ʌ	'dɛ.vən	mæn	ænd	ɾuld	ðʌ	'dɛ.vən	siz]

(Captain,	art	though	sleeping	there	below?)
['kæp.tən	ɑɐt	ðaːʊ	'slip.ɪŋ	ðɛɐ̯	bɪ.'loːʊ]

Roving	tho'	his	death	fell,	he	went	with	heart	at	ease,
['ɾoːʊv.ɪŋ	ðoːʊ	hɪz	dɛθ	fɛl	hi	wɛnt	wɪθ	hɑɐ̯t	æt	iz]

And **dreaming** **all** **the** **time** **of** **Plymouth** **Hoe.**
[ænd 'dɹim.ɪŋ ɑl ðʌ ta:ɪm ʌv 'plɪ.məθ ho:ʊ]

"Take **my** **drum** **to** **England,** **hang** **it** **by** **the** **shore,**
[te:ɪk ma:ɪ dɹʊm to:ʊ 'ɪŋ.glənd hæŋ ɪt ba:ɪ ðʌ ʃɔɐ̯]

Strike **it** **when** **your** **powder's** **running** **low;**
[stɹa:ɪk ɪt ʍɛn jʊɐ̯ 'pa:ʊ.dɐ̯z 'ɾʊ.nɪŋ lo:ʊ]

If **the** **Dons** **sight** **Devon,** **I'll** **quit** **the** **port** **of** **Heaven**
[ɪf ðʌ dɔnz sa:ɪt 'dɛ.vən a:ɪl kwɪt ðʌ po:ʊɐ̯t ʌv 'hɛ.vən]

And **drum** **them** **up** **the** **Channel** **as** **we** **drummed** **them** **long** **ago."**
[ænd dɹʊm ðɛm ʌp ðʌ 't͡ʃæ.nəl æz wi dɹʊmd ðɛm lɔŋ ə.'go:ʊ]

Drake **he's** **in** **his** **hammock** **till** **the** **great** **Armadas** **come,**
[dɹe:ɪk hiz ɪn hɪz 'hæ.mək tɪl ðə gɹe:ɪt aɾ.'ma.daz kʌm]

(Captain, **art** **though** **sleeping** **there** **below?)**
['kæp.tən aɐ̯t ða:ʊ 'slip.ɪŋ ðɛɐ̯ bə.'lo:ʊ]

Slung **atween** **the** **round** **shot** **list'ning** **for** **the** **drum,**
[slʊŋ ə'twin ðʌ ɾa:ʊnd ʃat 'lɪs.nɪŋ fɔɐ̯ ðʌ dɹʊm]

And **dreaming** **all** **the** **time** **of** **Plymouth** **Hoe.**
[ænd 'dɹi.mɪŋ ɑl ðʌ ta:ɪm ʌv 'plɪ.məθ ho:ʊ]

Call **him** **on** **the** **deep** **sea,** **Call** **him** **up** **the** **Sound,**
[kɔl hɪm ɔn ðʌ dip si kɔl hɪm ʌp ðʌ sa:ʊnd]

Call **him** **when** **ye** **sail** **to** **meet** **the** **foe;**
[kɔl hɪm ʍɛn ji se:ɪl tu mit ðʌ fo:ʊ]

Where **the** **old** **trade's** **plying** **and** **the** **old** **flag's** **flying,**
[ʍɛɐ̯ ði o:ʊld tɹe:ɪdz 'pla:ɪ.ɪŋ ænd ði o:ʊld flægz 'fla:ɪ.jɪŋ]

They **shall** **find** **him** **ware** **and** **waking,**
[ðe:ɪ ʃæl fa:ɪnd hɪm we:ɪɐ̯ ænd 'we:ɪk.ɪŋ]

As **they** **found** **him** **long** **ago!**
[æz ðe:ɪ fa:ʊnd hɪm lɔŋ ə.'go:ʊ]

Drake's Drum

Songs of the Sea, Op. 91

Henry Newbolt

Charles Villiers Stanford
(1852-1924)

Tempo di marcia moderato

Drake, he's in his ham-mock and a thou-sand mile a- way____

(Cap- tain, art thou sleep-ing there be-

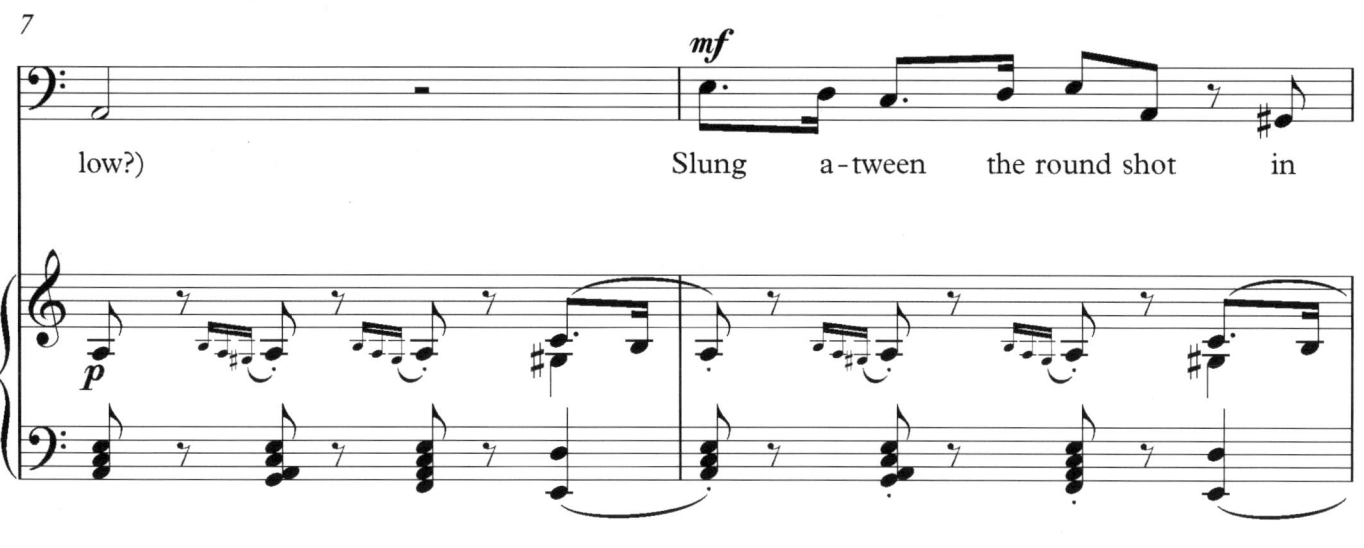

low?)   Slung a-tween the round shot in

Nom-bre Di - os Bay, And dream-ing all the time of Ply-mouth

Hoe.   Yon-der lumes the is-land yon-der lie the ships, With

sai - lor lads a - dan - cing heel - an' - toe And the

shore - lights flash-ing and the night - tide dash-ing, He sees it all so plain -

ly as he saw it long a - go.

Drake he was a De-von man, and ruled the De-von seas,_____

pp

(Cap - tain, art thou sleep-ing there be low?)

p

Rov - ing tho' his death fell, he went with heart at ease, And

dream-ing all the time of Ply-mouth Hoe.

"Take my drum to En-gland, hang it by the shore,

Strike it when your pow-der's run-ning low; If the

35

Dons sight De-von, I'll quit the port of Hea-ven And drum them up the Chan-nel as we

38

drummed them long a - go."

40
f largamente

Drake he's in his ham-mock till the

great Ar - ma - das come,

(Cap - tain, art thou sleep - ing there be -

low?) Slung a-tween the round shot

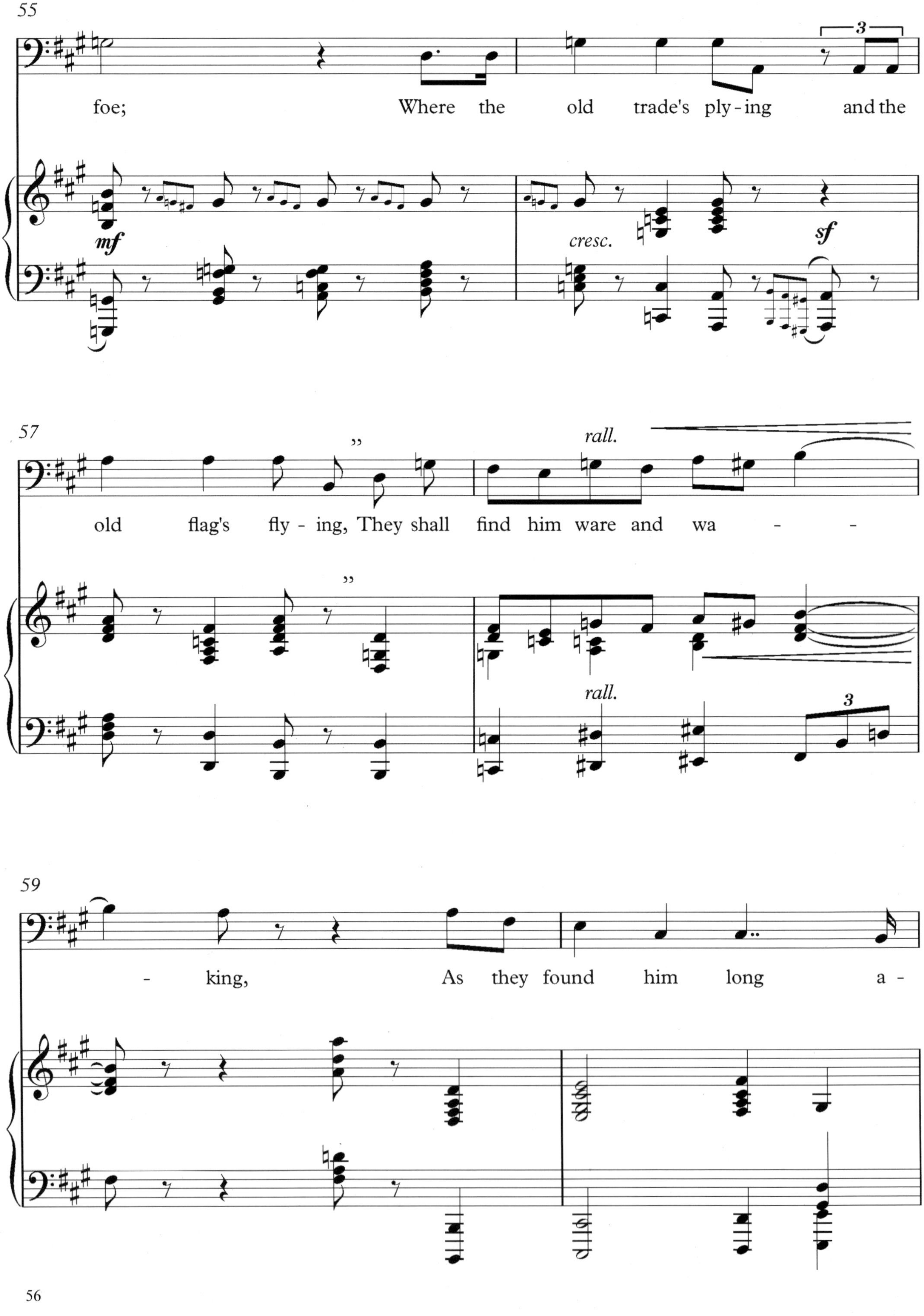
55
foe; Where the old trade's ply-ing and the
mf
cresc.
sf
57
old flag's fly - ing, They shall find him ware and wa - -
rall.
rall.
59
- king, As they found him long a -

O tu ch'innanzi morte

Aria from *Orfeo*
Claudio Monteverdi

Respiration and Support

Because the piece is in two/two meter and in an *adagio* tempo, it may be necessary to take more frequent breaths than might be expected. For example, insert a breath after *tu* and *temerario*.

Resonance

This melody often sits at the bottom of the staff. Take this opportunity to balance resonance and teach *chiaroscuro*. Sing with the lips together, the teeth apart and a long jaw with [m]. Notice sensations of resonance in the mask and the top of the head and the pharyngeal space that is gained.

Phonation

Vibrato rate in a young bass voice is sometimes too slow. To encourage vibrancy, trill the vocal line. Sing the trills, and then sing the vocal line without the trills with a feeling of motion in the voice.

Registration

The melody often descends from A^3, which is in the bass's first *passaggio*. To incorporate head voice at the top of the bass staff, sing descending sirens on [u]. Next, sing the melody with the same heady quality.

Siren on [u] to find head voice, so the melody can begin with the same quality.

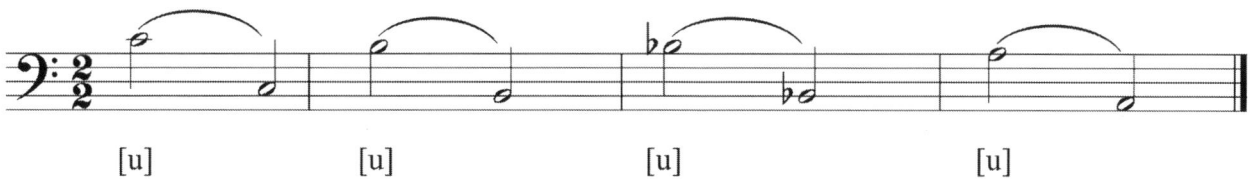

[u]   [u]   [u]   [u]

O   tu____ ch'in -nan - zi   mor - te a   que - ste   ri   -   ve

Diction/Articulation

The text of this piece offers ample opportunities to help young basses pronounce consonants with the lips, teeth and tongue.

Place a finger on the bottom lip while saying *shhh*. Notice the energy of the consonant. The jaw must remain flexible and unhinged. Speak the text through this flexible and unhinged position.

Phonetic Transcription and Translation of the Text

O tu ch'innanzi morte a queste rive
[o tu kin'nantsi 'mɔrte a 'kweste 'ri:ve]
Oh you, who before death, to these banks

temerato   ten' vieni, arresta i passi;
[teme'ra:rjo tɛn 'vjɛ:ni ar'rɛsta i 'passi]
boldy are coming, hold your steps;

Solcar quest'onde ad uom mortal non dassi,
[sol'kar kwe'stonde ad wɔ:m mɔr'ta:l non 'dassi]
Mortal man is not permitted to cut through these waves,

ne puo co' morti albergo aver chi vive.
[ne pwɔ ko 'mɔrti al'bɛrgo a've:r ki vi:.ve]
nor can the living seek shelter with the dead.

Che? Vuoi forse, nemico   al mio signore,
[ke   vwɔ:i 'fɔrse nɛ'mi:ko al mi:o siɲ'ɲo:re]
What? You wish maybe, enemy of my lord,

Cerbero trar da le tartaree porte?
[ˈtʃɛrbero traːr ˈdal.le tarˈtaːre ˈpɔrte]
to draw Cerberus away from the gates of hell?

O rapir brami sua cara consorte,
[o raˈpiːr ˈbramːmi suːa ˈkaːra konˈsɔrte]
Or do you desire to abduct his dear consort,

d'impudico desire acceso il core?
[dimpuˈdiːko deˈzire atˈtʃeːzo il ˈkɔːre]
since your heart is inflamed with wanton desire?

Pon freno al foll'ardir, ch'entr'al mio legno
[poːn ˈfreːno al ˈfɔlle arˈdiːr ˈkɛntral miːo ˈleɲɲo]
Refrain your foolish boldness, to enter my boat

non accorro piu mai corporea salma,
[non akkɔrˈrɔ pju maːi kɔrˈpɔːrea ˈsalma]
I will never again assist a living being,

sì de gli antichi oltaggi ancora ne l'alma
[si deʎ ʎanˈtiːke olˈtraddʒi aŋˈkoːr ne ˈlalma]
so much of the ancient wrongs still exist in my soul.

serbo acerba memoria e giusto sdegno.
[ˈsɛr.bo ˈa.ʃɛr.ba me.ˈmɔːrja e ˈdʒu.sto zdɛɲːɲo.]
I harbor harsh memories and righteous indignation.

O tu ch'innanzi morte

from *Orfeo*

Claudio Monteverdi
(1567-1643)

O tu___ ch'in-nan-zi mor - te a que-ste ri -
ve te-me - ra-rio t'en vie - ni, ar-re-sta i pas - si, sol-car que-st'on - de
ad uom mor-tal non das - si, né può có mor - ti al-ber - go a-ver chi

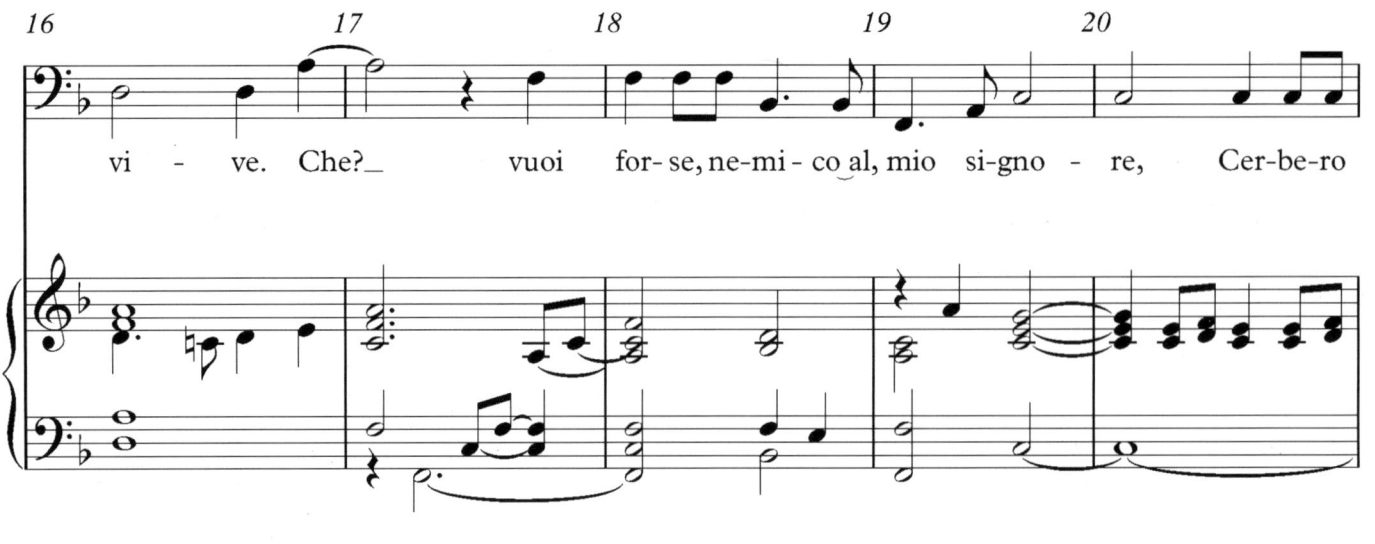

vi - ve. Che?__ vuoi for-se, ne-mi-co al, mio si-gno - re, Cer-be-ro

trar___ da le tar-ta - ree por - te? O ra-pir bra - mi sua ca-ra con-sor -

te, d'im-pu - di-co de-si-re ac-ce - so il co - re? Pon fre-

- no al fol-le ar-dir, ch'en - tr'al mio le - gno non ac-cor - rò più mai cor -

po - rea sal - ma, sì de gli an-ti-chi ol-trag-gi an-cor ne l'al - ma ser -

bo a - cer-ba me-mo - ria e giu-sto sde - gno.

rit.

Befraget mich ein zartes Kind

Aria from *Bastien und Bastienne*
Wolfgang Amadeus Mozart

Respiration and Support

The opening vocal lines of this piece include frequent rests, followed by longer, legato phrases. This provides an excellent opportunity to teach breath coordination. The abdominal muscles are released on rests.

Pulse the abdominal muscles to the rhythms of the vocalises given. The abdominal muscles move in on the pitches and release on the rests.

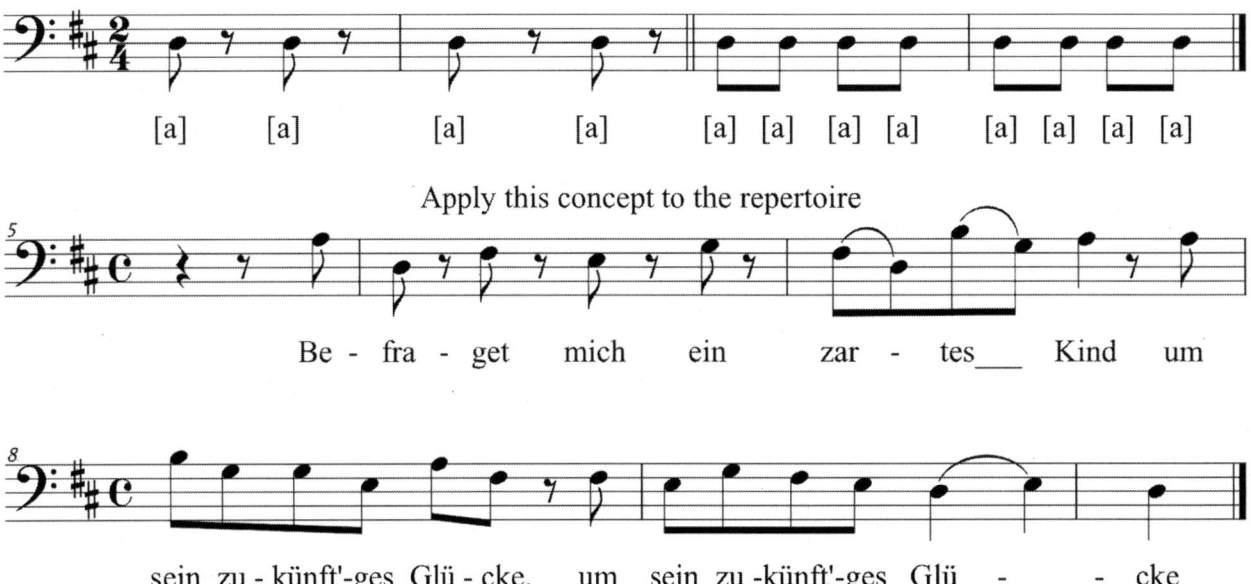

Resonance

This passage is tricky because of the juxtaposed vowels that are similar but distinct. Instruct the student to alternate the vowels [ʏ] and [ə].

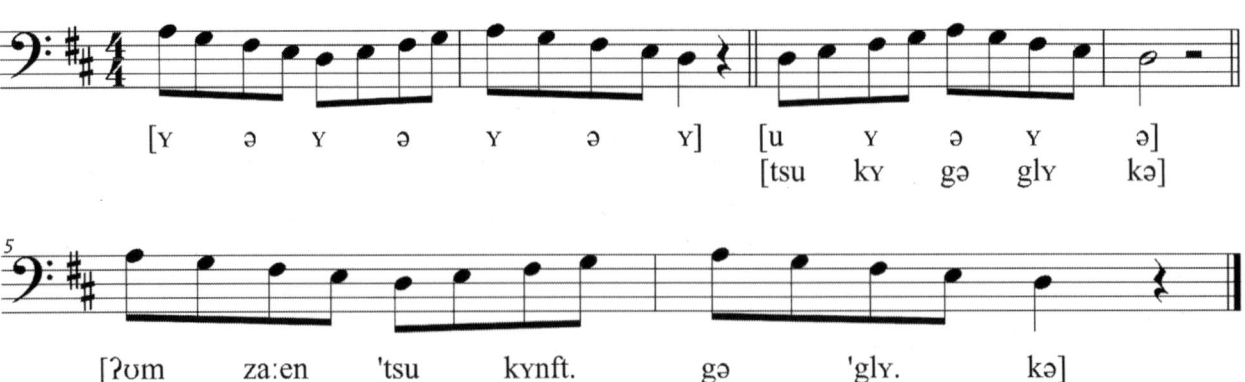

Phonation

There are many words that begin with vowels in this aria, which require a gentle glottal onset in the German language. Use a silent cough in the shape of the following vowels to practice a gentle glottal onset:

[ɪ]
[a]
[ʊ]

Registration

[g] helps to influence a flexible, low laryngeal position. Practice singing the vocal line on [gu].

Use this vocalise to prepare for difficulties in registration.

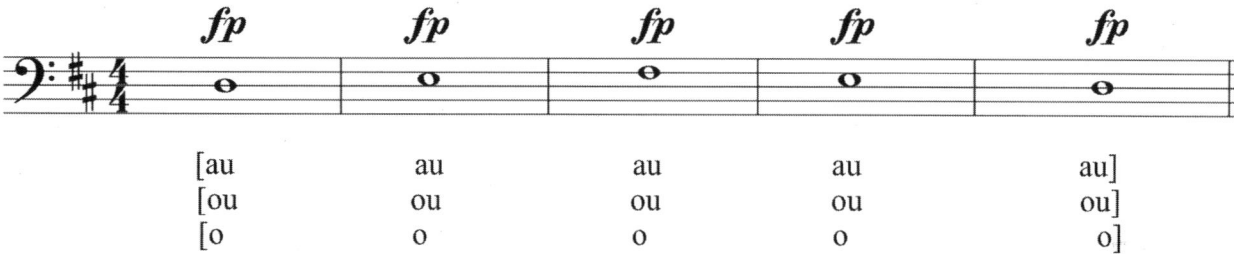

Diction/Articulation

A challenging aspect of articulation in this piece is the quick alternation of sibilants. Instruct the student to pulse on each individual consonant, then practice the consonants in the order in which they appear in the text.

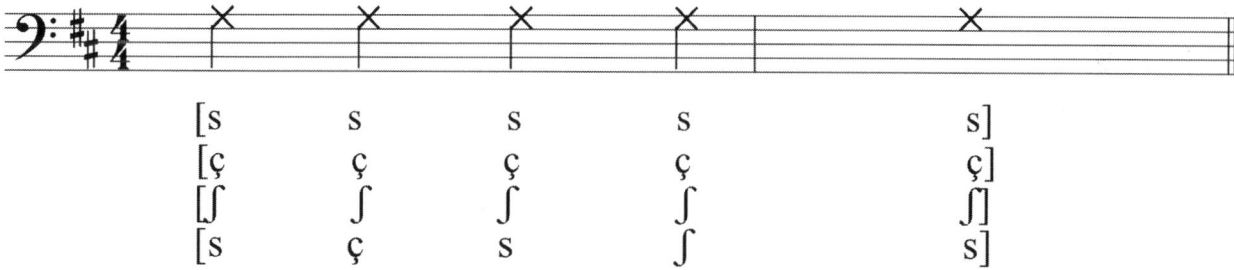

Phonetic Transcription and Translation of the Text

Befraget   mich   ein   zartes   Kind
[bə.ˈfraː.gət   mɪç   ʔaːen   ˈtsar.təs   kɪnt]
If a young girl asks me

um   sein   zukünft'ges   Glücke,
[ʔʊm   zaːen   ˈtsu.kʏnft.gəs   ˈglʏ.kə]
about her fortune,

les'   ich   das   Schicksal   ihm   geschwind
[leːs   ʔɪç   das   ˈʃɪk.zaːl   ʔiːm   gə.ˈʃvɪnt]
I can see her fate quickly

aus   dem   verliebten   Blicke.
[ʔaːos   deːm   fɛ̯.ˈliːp.tən   ˈblɪ.kə]
from the look of love on her face,.

Ich   sehe,   bloß   des   Liebsten   Gunst
[ʔɪç   ˈzeː.ə   ˈbloːs   dɛs   ˈliːps.tən   gʊnst]
I see, only her beloved's favor

Kann   zum   Vergnügen   taugen.
[kan   tsum   fɛ̯.ˈgnyː.gən   ˈtaːu.gən]
can bring true happiness

Wie   leicht   wird   mir   die   Zauberkunst
[viː   laːeçt   vɪrt   miːɐ̯   di   ˈtsaːubɐ.ˌkʊnst]
How easy the magical art is for me,

bei   zwei   verliebten   Augen.
[baːe   tsvaːe   fɛ̯.ˈliːp.tən   ˈʔaːu.gən]
to read two love-filled eyes.

Befraget mich ein zartes Kind

Bastien und Bastienne

F.W. Weiskern,
J.H. F. Müller,
and J.A. Schachtner

W.A. Mozart
(1756-1791)

Be - fra - get mich ein zar - tes___ Kind um

sein zu-künft' - ges Glü-cke, um sein zu-künft' - ges Glü - cke, les'

ich das Schick - sal ihm ge - schwind aus dem ver-lieb-ten Bli - cke,

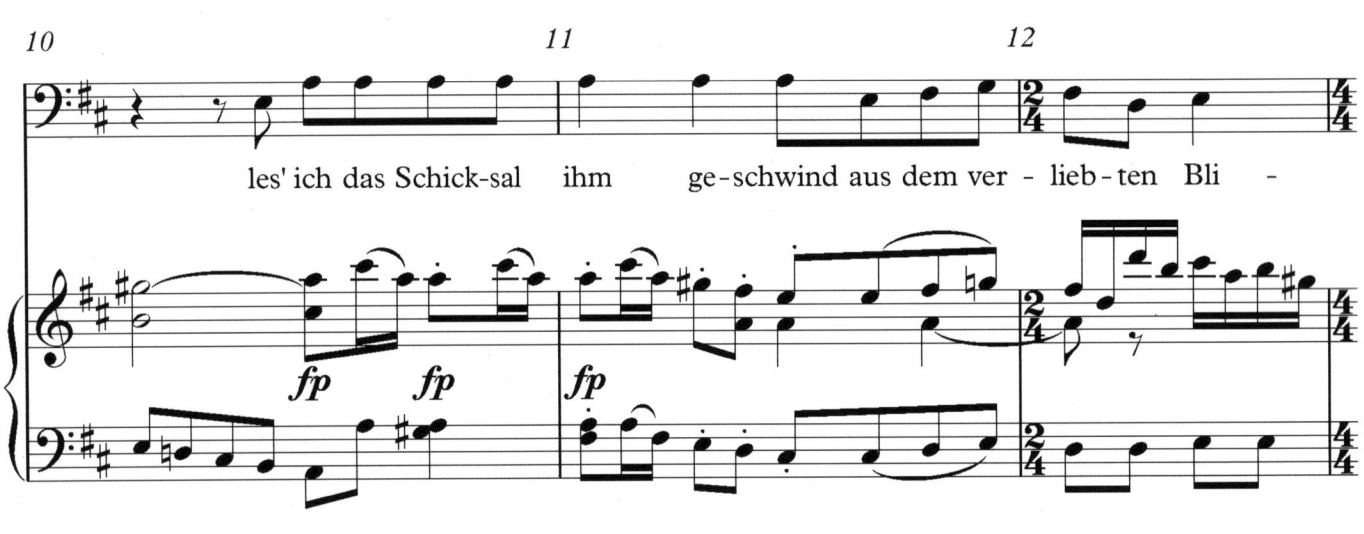

les' ich das Schick-sal ihm ge-schwind aus dem ver - lieb-ten Bli -

cke, aus dem ver - lieb - ten Bli - - cke.

Ich se - he, bloß des Lieb-sten Gunst kann zum Ver-gnü-gen tau-

gen. Ich se - he, bloß des Lieb-sten Gunst kann zum Ver-gnü-gen tau-

gen Wie leicht wird mir die Zau-ber-kunst bei

zwei ver - lieb - ten Au - gen,

p *cresc.* *f* *p*

bei

zwei ver - lieb - ten Au - - - gen!

Sample Rubric for Grading Repertoire

Scale of 1-5
0-20 points easy, 20-40 points moderate, 40-60 points difficult

Technical Issue Addressed	Problem Solving Questions	Scale 1-5
ACCOMPANIMENT	Is the accompaniment utilitarian, supportive, independent, etc.? Is the accompaniment part of the story line? Descriptive e.g. water figures, spinning wheel, etc.?	
CHARACTERIZATION/ACTING	Is the character appropriate to the student's dramatic capacity or life experiences? Will the student benefit from portraying this type of character?	
DICTION/ARTICULATION	Consideration of challenging consonant clusters. Closed position or difficult consonants on challenging pitches? Student's knowledge of French, Italian, Russian, German, etc. language or diction?	
DYNAMICS	Is the singer expected to sing a pianissimo high note? Are the markings pedagogically helpful (e.g. crescendo on sustained notes to assist in breath energy and/or vibrancy?)	
MELISMATIC PHRASES	Beginner or advanced melismas/melismatic phrases present? Appoggiatura? Dotted rhythms?	
MUSICAL CONSIDERATIONS	Through composed? Strophic? Accessible harmonic language? Tonal? An enjoyable melody?	
RANGE/TESSITURA	How are high notes approached—dramatically? Is the range too vast? Is the tessitura too low or high? Can a young singer sit in that particular part of the voice for that long without fatiguing?	
REGISTRATION	Does the piece assist in working through *passaggio* issues? Will the student carry weight up? Helpful vowels in an underdeveloped part of the student's voice? Etc.	
RESPIRATION	Are phrase lengths accessible? Will the breaths allow for renewal of positioning?	
TEXT SETTING	Syllabic, Patter Song, Lyric? Does the text setting assist in memorization?	
VOWELS/VOWEL SEQUENCES	Observation of vowels in *passaggio*. Will vowel patterns assist in correcting vocal faults forward to back, tongue position, etc.?	
WORDS: POETRY/LYRICS/LIBRETTO	Is this accessible poetry? Is the story age appropriate? Will the text make the memorization process difficult?	